JUST BEYOND YOUR EXPOSURE

The Art of Manage Human Resources

Dr. Allan P. Miller LLB., B.HR., P.hD

VOLUME ONE

Published by New Generation Publishing in 2023

Copyright © 2022 Dr. Allan P. Miller

Front cover design by Dr. Allan P. Miller

First published in Longwood: Florida, Xulon Press, USA 2007

ISBN: 978-1-60266-552-1

www.newgeneration-publishing.com

 New Generation Publishing

DEDICATION

This study is dedicated to all the students and staffs of the different HR Institution. Also to all the staffs over the years that I worked with in management at the Public, Private and Voluntary Sector organisational setting.

To {of DR. P. G. Powell/
MAy the blessing of God be with
Tou and Tour family Always
4/4/2023

PREFACE

In the past years most people expected to enter a job, possibly by means of an apprenticeship and then to remain in that job for most of their working life. Things have changed. In today's increasingly global and competitive environment the effective management of people is even more important for organisations survival and success. I am happy with what you have written, especially on jobs becoming a series of short-term contracts.

The nature of Dr. Allan Miller, book "JUST BEYOND YOUR EXPOSURE: The Art of Manage Human Resources" and the practice of management should be considered not in a vacuum but within an organisation's context and environment. Private / public organisations find these types of contracts low in price, liabilities and commitments. In order to attain a reasonable depth, this book concentrates on twelve selected topics of particular relevance to problems of organisation and the management of people in the work situations, and which meet the needs of the intended audience.

Notes: little or no job security and the subsequent obstacles and benefits arising from these changes to work practices, for both the employee and employer. Recognises that this effectiveness of "JUST BEYOND YOUR EXPOSURE:

The Art of Manage Human Resources", depends very largely upon the staffs it employs.

Dr. Miller draws attention to the importance of the promotion of good human relations for improved organisations performance. Dr. Allan Miller has open and closes a tin determination and achievement. The range is incredible.

This book of twelve chapters is logically structured and clearly written, with the academic integrity. Will not only appeal to those aspiring to managerial positions, but to practising managers, supervisors, students, teachers who wish to expand their views and knowledge of the subject area. For this, I congratulate him.

Joan Chance, Ph. D
Manager of Social Service, London: England

FORWARD

In these days, we are face with challenges of different kinds within the job world, which call for organisational leadership of all kinds to be better prepares to face these challenges. The very same way just as a skilled carpenter gathers the right tools for the job at hand, a skilled leader, manager and preacher also fills his or her toolbox with critical knowledge, skills, and attitudes that fit the job to be done. When that job involves building effective organisation, the individual toolbox must contain knowledge about what organisation are, when and why they should be used, and how they can be organized to maximize their effectiveness.

In creating effective organisational, Dr. Miller, goal was to create a toolbox filled with just what you need most to became an effective member and leader or even a preacher in the organization. But the content of his author book is practical and realistic, yet drawn from various individual, students and different organisational experiences members who make this book both scholarly and profoundly.

Now the author of this book Rev. Dr. Miller, whose bestselling book has helped tens of hundreds of people conquer the clutter in their lives, explains how to overcome the "JUST BEYOND YOUR EXPOSURE: The Art of Manage Human Resources", the organisational leadership challenges once and for all.

His ground-breaking from-the-inside-out approach will help you uncover your psychological, strengths and stumbling block and create a better leadership system that suits your individual need.

Additionally, these chapters one of the most crucial organisational and leadership skills in this age of information – recognized the valve and subsequent individuals and people have confirmed, that learning organisational or HR fulfil several essential functions that are especially beneficial to all at large. Congratulation to you again Rev. Dr. Allan Miller, to enhance and expand this book with a dynamic utterance, that contains an abundance of rich and beneficial success.

C. H. Blackwale, BSC (HR)
Consultation

ENDORSEMENT

In those institutions which are just developing the personnel role there is usually highly centralised personnel function whose main duty is to promote the development and growth of this function. Dr. Miller is well known and respected as a Bible teacher, preacher and mentor, in our Pentecostal Churches. He has been accredited as a rare example of a Pentecostal Theologian, minister, counsellor and educator, who is willing to share his wealth of experience and knowledge with younger ministers, teachers, managers, etc. Dr. Miller teaching ministry has positively impacted and transformed many individuals, in all walks of life, regardless of their race or colour – Black or White or their level of intellectual ability.

His writings are always motivating, inspiring, challenging and practical, which this book "JUST BEYOND YOUR EXPOSURE: The Art of Manage Human Resources", is no less intellectual, informative, motivating and inspiring. Dr. Allan P. Miller has demonstrated, with profound clarity, that the teaching of how to manage (HR) is imperative, not only for the present effective leadership, but also for the future leadership of the different organisation and even the Bible Colleges. His teaching has powerfully impacted and influenced many who might never have had an opportunity to achieve.

Generally, writing a book can be very stressful. This is especially true in writing a text book, such as this, for students, managers, supervisor and counselling Church leaders. Dr. Miller insight into (HR) is powerful, challenging, and analytical sound. It is profoundly and indescribably a work of splendour and an in-depth study to which every potential and even veteran leaders, can turn for a long time to come.

Reshma Chambers, BA (Hons), MA in HRM
Consultation of Deloitte MCS Ltd
London: England

ACKNOWLEDGEMENT

First and foremost, praises and thanks to the God, the Almighty, for His showers of blessings throughout my research work, and for helping me to complete the research successfully. I would like to express my deep and sincere gratitude to my supervisor and mentor Rev Dr G. A. Christopher. His dynamism, vision, sincerity and motivational grace have deeply inspired me. He has taught me the methodology to carry out the research and to present the research works as clearly as possible. It was a great privilege and honour to work and study under his guidance. I am extremely grateful for what he has offered me.

Besides my mentor, I would like to extend my heartfelt thanks to Rev Prof Isaac Ojutalayo, Professor, for his encouragements to reprint and update this book for the course study discussion for different management field. Moreover, his timely and scholarly advice, meticulous scrutiny and scientific methodology have helped me to a great extent to accomplish this task.

There is no way to acknowledge all of them, but I want to been particularly helpful. I would like to express my sincere gratitude to Blackwale, Chamber, Dr. Chance for all faithful support, vision and guidance have helped me throughout the period of my research and writing of this book for reprinting.

Lastly, but not least, I am extremely grateful to all my parents, for their love, prayers, care and sacrifice for educating and preparing me for my future. I am very much thankful to my brothers and sisters, wife and children for their love, understanding, prayers, and continuing support towards the completion of this research work.

CONTENTS

SUMMARY

This study describes some of detail the principles of good practice which are common across the different sectors and which cannot be sufficiently well described in the detail of other studies. This therefore, relates to and is closely bound with all other legislation. This is because the principles of good practice should directly influence and mould how you undertake all the rest of your work activities. I believe that every local authority is seeking to make more consistent the way departmental service strategies are produced and how will eventually lock into the community plan allocate. As you will see, nothing I have discussed was really peculiar or specific to industry or to the private sector. Leadership is, after all, largely an issue of people and their ability to communicate effectively with one another. We all, with varying degrees of success, manage their finances.

Often the changes you have to implement are important to the survival or success of your organisation. They involve the different technology that the organisations need to be competitive. The new structure needs to be effective and the reduced level of overhead needs to be profitable. There is no one who cannot greatly improve their leadership through a little extra thought and practice, as the young manager in this book has proved. People are seen as a responsibility and a resource to be added to. I have been involved directly in studies for some years at different educational institutions, and have observed that each has its own interest in beliefs. During this period, I have come across countless number of students and numerous articles, including books on the subject with different types of beliefs. From my experience in these various studies, I have chosen this title for this research. My study consists of eleven chapters, summarized as follows:

Chapter One (The Nature of Organisational Setting): as we approach a different century, one problem continues and perhaps even magnifies itself in the Organisational Setting all around us. The drives innovations create better experience for customers and enables employees to make faster and smarter business decisions. It's about becoming an operation that is resilient and able to respond to change at the right time.

Chapter Two (Operating Model for Organisational Theory and Design): This is focused on addressing the problems which are the central elements in the understanding of leadership or management style that cause people and organisational changes. This research also aims at providing theoretical and practical suggestions which will enable us to have a greater ability to recognize and provide valuable resources to help cost effectiveness.

Chapter Three (A Configuration Model of Organisational Cultural Theory): this study has a strong focus on the singularity of organisational groups with suggestions on how to manage mental challenges with the critical capabilities of achieving excellent qualities to help an organisation. These are all important, and I have taken them into consideration throughout the process of this study.

Chapter Four (The Nature of Organisational Behaviour): this chapter discusses a fundamental programmer designed to help create a more robust system to help transform the nature of organisational behaviour. The core objective is to help us develop a more future proofed operating model, by using our organisational frame work which assesses all elements of the internal and external operating model.

Chapter Five (Understanding the Roles in Organisational Skills): we should be more confident that we have the optimal organisational architecture to help implement and provide valuable resources to our customers and achieve better results. So, what have we learned about being an effective team members and leaders? What do we need to learn about how our organisation can improve the quality team members? This chapter discusses these inquiries.

Chapter Six (The Importance of Teamwork in the Organisational Setting): As we move into a future where many organisations are embracing the process of management working as a team and building activities, we will witness more organisations becoming more satisfied with their political implementation and keep their team members connected are the basic rules discussed in this chapter.

Chapter Seven (Types of Communication Theories in the Organisational Setting): When it comes to digital transformation there is no before and after. It's a very good journey that requires an understanding organisation to take part on the right shapes, in support of its people and its ambitions. Our communication operating model solutions are stress tested, providing certainty armful to Miller's Bible

College and Institution. The positive changes experienced by this institution are highlighted in this thesis.

Rev. Dr. Allan P. Miller

Chapter One
The Nature of Organisational Setting

Definitions of Organisation Sector

This chapter has reviewed three ways in which smart city activity, whether led by local companies, local government, or local voluntary sector organizations, can deepen the participation of local groups in smart city projects and visions. Initiatives such as symmetrisation and modularisation are now common in higher education. The questions, assignments and case studies provide an opportunity to relate ideas, principles and practices to specific work situations, to think and talk about major issues, and to discuss and compare views with colleagues. In order to help relate the contents of the chapters to real-life situations, many of the questions and assignments ask you to support your discussion with, and / or to give, examples from your own organisation. This can of course be your own college or college department. Alternatively, you may have work experience, even part-time or casual employment, in other organisations that you may draw upon and share with colleagues.

In all three areas of activity, a consistent theme has been the importance of engaging with local organizations, local priorities, and local knowledge of place. This study adopts and applies approach to the search for the most appropriate ways of improving organisational performance and effectiveness. The objective analysis of organisations is supported, where appropriate, by a more prescriptive stance. For example, local actors have long experience of their city and often have a great deal of insight into how it could be made better. Drawing on that expertise is surely a fundamental success factor that will ensure that the deployment of digital technologies will indeed make cities better places to live in. General principles and prescriptions apply equally to all types of work organisations which achieve their goals and objectives through the process of management.

Ann Gravells wrote:

> The further education and skills sector, previously known as the lifelong learning sector, includes those aged 14 and upwards who are in:
> - Adult education
> - Armed, emergency and uniformed services
> - Charitable organisations
> - Community education
> - Further education colleges
> - Higher education institutions and universities
> - Immigration and detention centres
> - Private sector learning
> - Probation services
> - Public and private training organisations
> - Schools and academies
> - Voluntary sector learning
> - Work-based learning. [1]

Although there is a logical flow to the sequencing of topic areas, each part and each chapter of the study is self-contained. Accordingly, you may come across sectors that are aimed at helping us work towards the requirements of the mission, goals, vision or award in theory and practice. If we are into a managerial position locally, nationally or internationally, some of the regulations and organisations referred in this study may not be applicable to the nation or country in which we work. Perhaps we have a hobby or a trade we would like to teach others; we know we are good at it and feel we have the skills and knowledge which we could pass on to others. Depending upon where and what we are going to teach or manage, we may not need to be qualified in our particular subject, but we should be able to demonstrate appropriate skills and knowledge at a particular level.

The effective management of people takes place in the context of the wider environmental setting, including the changing patterns of organisations and attitudes to work. It is frequently documented that a global economy, increased business competitiveness, the move towards more customer-driven markets, advances in scientific knowledge, especially telecommunications and office automation, and the downsizing of organisations have led to a period of constant change and the need for greater organisational flexibility. This could seem to be a recurring theme currently in United States, Asia, United Kingdom and Jamaica. It is required that we have level above that which we will teach or manage in our organisational sectors, for example, if we are new to teaching, this could be because we are contemplating a change of profession, or we are required to take a particular teaching qualification because of our job role.

According to A. Hudson, D. Hayes and T. Andrew:

> Organisations are making increasing use of group or team approaches to work with an emphasis on co-operation, participation and empowerment. A recent attitude to work survey found a preoccupation with education and training as a way to get on in life or at least to survive in the labour market. However, although responsibility is accepted, it is often seen as an unwanted imposition and there is a feeling of helplessness among many people in their work environment. [2]

The power and influence of public, private and voluntary organisations, the rapid spread of new technology, and the impact of various socio-economic and political factors have given rise to the concept of corporate social responsibilities and business ethics. Increasing attention is being focused on the ethical behaviour which underlies the decisions and actions of managers and staff; and many responsible organisations and professional bodies now choose to publish a code of ethics.

According to Dick Benjamin, the founder of Abbott loops Christian Centre in Anchorage:

> What a privilege! To know God! There is no higher calling on the face of the earth than to actually walk and talk with God and to have

Him talk to you. God talks to men; He really desires this intimate communion. People are really missing out in the Christian life if they're just going through the motions of religious ceremony. The church organisation as a sector is the house where God dwells. Just as in your business, school and human household, if I entered the house (sector) and ignored the man of the house, something would be drastically wrong. [3]

The changing nature of organisations and individuals at work has placed increasing pressure on the awareness and importance of new psychological contracts. There to help employees improve their knowledge and skills; and others are to help people improve their confidence or health and wellbeing. There are many programmes available for different reasons or to fulfil certain needs, for examples, it is important to note here what we mean by "local." Clearly, very little that happens in Jamaica, United States, United Kingdom etc., is confined to inside the city or country. They are designed to help every organization involved in smart city projects in the city on countries is also embedded in institutional networks with regional, national, and in some cases international reach. Ideas and activities emerge from the city and flow out from it, and ideas and projects arrive in the city from elsewhere. Some of these connections and relations are deeply embedded, others provisional and temporary.

However, places are also different. The most important aspect of managing the organisational sectors is to ensure that learning is taking place. If we are currently teaching or managing one of the sectors, our delivery methods might be based on experiences of how we were taught in the past. However, there are many different approaches we could use, specially like in the covid19 in a more engaging and motivating way. It isn't just about delivering to groups in a classroom style; it can take place in many different environments such as training in the workplace, public, private or voluntary settings, delivering sessions indoors, outdoors, or online.

Laurie J. Mullins wrote:

> When you get down to it, an e-business is an organisation that connects critical business systems directly to their customers, employees, partners and suppliers, via intranets, extranets and over the web. As customers, employees, suppliers and distributors are all connected to the business systems and information they need e-business actually transforms and integrates key business processes. In short, the definition of e-business is: the transformation of key business processes using internet technologies. [4]

Organisations of all sizes are impacted by globalisation and deregulation, which lowers barriers to entry and dramatically reshapes the competitive landscape. People now have a broader array of choices and therefore are becoming more sophisticated and more demanding public, private and voluntary sectors - in what they want from a supplier but also how they choose to acquire goods and services. Thus, the need to their funding and governance structures is different. For example, United State and United Kingdom itself has a particular history as a new town which, as this chapter has briefly noted, has contributed to a particular local social landscape of many quite active community groups and organizations. This intellectual capital is a most valuable asset, but only when it is leveraged for competitive advantage. This has shaped this chapter's account of how to make smart projects work better.

Also—and perhaps more importantly—the city has a hegemonic narrative that describes itself as forward-looking and innovative. They have a strong sense that United States or United Kingdom from its foundation have been a sort of urban experiment and that it had a long history of trailing a range of innovative urban technologies, from solar-powered housing to cable television to smart dustbins. This sense of the particularity of them, what one of our interviewees called its "sense of get up and go, we can do it," is also part of the why and how of local engagement in smart.

According to Jim Durkin and Dick Iverson, the different units to the value will give a good idea of what it likes to teach or manage. You can then take a further teaching or managerial qualification if required:

> It was on the road to Damascus that Paul pursued his mission to capture and imprison Christians that his life course was suddenly interrupted by a visible encounter with the Lord Jesus Christ. He had spent most of his life previous to this in dedicated training and service within the Jewish religious system. This startled Doctor of the Law would now

be forced into a total re-examination of his
existing convictions and directions. ₅

We could substitute alongside questions about the
geographies of provision are questions about the
accessibility and inclusivity of what is available. Services
may be perceived in socially exclusive ways, despite
apparent intentions to the contrary. The geography of
provision and inclusivity of psychotherapy services is
further complicated by matters of confidentiality, and fears
about visual exposure and stigmatization.

For example, some people from minority ethnic groups
prefer to see a practitioner from any ethnic background
other than their own; some people refuse to use services
where their attendance might be observed by people they
know; some service users prefer to travel considerable
distances rather than using otherwise more convenient
services in their own residential localities. Services respond
with lavational strategies, such as sitting in multi-use
buildings, and by resisting restrictions on access based on
tightly drawn geographical boundaries.

Ann Gravells wrote:

> Professional boundaries are those within
> which you need to work and it's important not
> to overstep these, for example, by becoming
> too personal or friendly with your learners.
> You should be able to work within the limits
> of that role, but know that it's okay to ask for
> help. Don't try to take on too much, or carry

out something which is part of someone else's role. 6

Most rational decisions are based on some form of theory. Theory helps in building generalised models applicable to a range of organisations or situations. So, if we are looking for that kind of employment, we may consider opportunities into one of three the public or private and voluntary sectors. However, to be of any help to the practising manager, theory has to be appropriate. Although it is not always easy to establish their exact origins, ideas do percolate through to best practice.

Laurie J. Mullins made these statements:

> There are a variety of types of case studies and they may be presented in a number of different ways. Case studies range from, for example, a brief account of events which may be actual, contrived or a combination of both; armchair cases based on hypothetical but realistic situations, and developed to draw out and illustrate particular points of principle; to complex, multi-dimensional cases giving a fuller descriptive account of actual situations in real organisations. The term case study may be extended to include critical incident analysis, role-play and the in-tray exercise, although these are more methods of training. 7

Whatever the nature or form of case studies, a major objective of their use is usually the application of theoretical knowledge to practical situations and / or the integration of knowledge drawn from a number of related disciplines or areas of study. There is unlikely to be a single, right answer to the 'voluntary sector' refers to organisations whose primary purpose is to create social impact rather than profit. It is often called the third sector, civil society or the not-for-profit sector. While the public sector provides services to the public, the private sector focuses on the interests of individual organizations and their stakeholders. When you understand each sector and its advantages, you can determine which of the two suits your needs and interests best.

The Private Sector Organisation
While working towards our mission, vision, goal or award, it would be extremely beneficial for us to have a mentor, someone who can help and support us, not only with teaching and managerial skills, but also with our specialist subject knowledge. Conversely, we could observe them to gain useful ideas and tips for the private sector represent the segment of the economy owned and operated by individuals and for-profit companies. Unlike one of the public sectors, defined as companies in the private sector, which represents are not government-owned or operated. It can be useful to summarise to create an action plan for my future development.

According to Laurie J. Mullins:

> The extent of the state ownership of public sector operations, or of their privatisation, and the balance between commercial and social interests, are determined by the government of the day. In recent years, there has been a

vigorous policy of creating freedom from state control and the transfer of business undertakings to private hands. The distinction can be made private enterprise organisations are owned and financed by individuals, partners, or shareholders in a joint stock company and are accountable to their owners or members. They vary widely in nature and size, and the type and scope of goods and services provided. [8]

Private sector employees typically receive more opportunities for job advancement because the decision is based on their performance. In the public sector, such decisions may rely on government regulations or rules. Once we have made the decision, we need to research what jobs are available for the amount of time we are able to commit. For example, we might like to give up our current career full place of work. The secret of success lies in the way private sectors have shaken up the corporate culture, and made public servants who had no incentive to serve their customers into effective managers willing to take risks in order to run their operations more efficiently or make a profit. D. Smith wrote:

Although the private – public sector divide is part of the British economic and political landscape, the divisions are being broken down and moves between the two sectors – in both directions – becoming more frequent. Business people are being introduced to the public sector in an unprecedented way and bringing their expertise to bear on efficiency across Whitehall. [9]

Part of the rationale for this development is that these organisations have expertise and competencies which are not as well developed in the public sector. This has facilitated the private sector positions; this will differ depending upon the demand for our particular subject. We will need to be prepared to put in time of our own. Even though we might feel we get a good hourly rate of pay, we have to take into account that this covers us for all the work we do which is outside of these hours. Our problems testify not so much to our inability to perform publicly as to our inability to get along with people in private, interpersonal relations.

Kenneth O. Gangel wrote:

> As we approach the end of the century, one problem continues and perhaps even magnifies itself in the leadership vacuum all around us. That problem centres in a misunderstanding of leadership style that causes people and organisations to focus on individuals. ...even secular literature has seen a strong movement away from the singularity of leadership, the strong person who possesses qualities to lead an organization. [10]

In terms of payment, private sector employees have more opportunities for pay raises and higher salaries than their public sector counterparts. One reason is that some high-level public sector jobs have income caps, while private-sector jobs do not. Like promotions, a private sector company can increase an employee's salary based on their work performance. But what kind of administrative structure facilitates cross-communication and interchange among various sub-systems? One reason many new private organisation sectors grow quickly may lie in the sense of community that early participants build with each other.

Kenneth O. Gangel made this statement

> Edwards Deming shook the corporate world to its very boardrooms a few years ago with his concept of total quality management. A systematic approach to analyzing the functions of any private sector organisation, total quality management emphasizes wide-angle thinking and decision making. Deming stressed that we must view systems as wholes, since a piecemeal approach will not produce. The only way to change a private sector organisation is to view it as a whole and acknowledge the team leadership that collectively determines its future. [11]

The private sector offers greater diversity in job opportunities, allowing individuals to find works based on their varying interests. The public sector has existing agencies and organizations focused on providing specific public services, which may offer more limited options.

The Public Sector Organisation
When we are with our learner (employee), we should always use clear language at an appropriate level and in terms they will understand. Although manager and other staffs know

what they are talking about, this might be the first time your employees have heard it, therefore never be afraid of repeating yourself or going over aspects again. I have found this to be more important than in the public sector – that is, the segment of the economy owned and operated by the government than in the private sector. Public sector employees typically enjoy more job stability because their organizations do not need to meet market pressures. These employees also often perform services that are consistently needed by the public, which can further ensure job safety.

Laurie J. Mullins mention:

> Public sector organisations are created by government and include, for example, municipal undertakings and central government departments, which do not have profit as their goal. Municipal undertakings such as local authorities are 'owned' by the council tax payers and ratepayers and financed by council taxes, rates, government grants, loans and charges for certain services. Central government departments are 'state owned' and financed by funds granted by parliament. Public sector organisations have political purposes and do not distribute profits. Any surplus of revenue over expenditure may be reallocated by improved services or reduced charges. The main aim is a service to and the well-being of the community. 12

Individuals working for government agencies or departments often receive comprehensive benefits packages. These benefits may include health insurance and retirement benefits. This advantage can make it easy for such employees to move amongst different public sector jobs while retaining similar benefits. In a helpful article Bob Welch reminds us:

> Job descriptions should be reviewed annually by the employee...any changes in job descriptions should be done mutually by the employee and the administration. It is a good idea to make a notation with any changes, acknowledging that both parties agreed to them. This will diminish the possibility of future confusion and disagreement. Clearly written, up-to-date and effective job descriptions tell an applicant your sector is both organized and efficient. They provide confidence, stability, and accountability related to employee actions and interactions. Finally, they facilitate positive staff relationships, making time spent on job descriptions time well spent. 13

Some individuals may enjoy the public sector because it can provide opportunities to serve the community. Rather than striving to create profits, they can play a role in improving the lives of others. They don't need to know anything personal about you, but they will probably make assumptions about you. If asked personal questions, if you try to remain a professional, and not becoming too friendly, you will retain respect. These organizations typically do not seek profit and often provide public services to the government's citizens. Some of the advantages of working in the public sector include:

Key differences between the public and private sectors
The public and private sectors sometimes partner to complete goals, such as construction or transportation projects. Examples like when person flying an airplane years ago.

Jim Durkin wrote:

> Pilots of small plans planes had to fly by visual flight rules. This meant that after take-off, the plane had to be oriented in the right direction by some visual landmark. While the compass could point the general direction, it was not reliable. Being magnetic, the compass needle would tend to sway. It couldn't provide steady direction because of its short-term gyrations. If a pilot tried to follow it strictly, he might never reach his destination, especially if fuel was limited. To keep on a straight and steady flight path, I was taught how to pick out a visual landmark, perhaps a mountain or some other feature that could be seen fifty miles out on the horizon. By keeping my eyes fixed on that landmark, I could keep the plane steady and moving straight toward a long-range destination. [14]

I use this analogy because it so clearly illustrates the effect of both public and private sectors short or long-term perspective; one is choppy, erratic and wastes fuel; the other guides the plane on a steady, constant and certain course. Any individual without a long-term perspective in public or private sectors will follow the same pattern. Instead of moving with steadiness and certainty special in covid19, it will continually swerve off course. There is an endless supply of distractions that will take sectors off the course of pursuing purpose, goal and vision. There are more private businesses than public sector businesses, meaning there are naturally more job opportunities for people in the private sector than in the public sector. Despite this, there are multiple job roles that can be found across both sectors, including in healthcare, broadcasting, and banking.

Hrand Faxenian wrote an article several years ago in which he places the responsibility for such communication on the leader. He said:

> You encourage your people to communicate effectively first by setting the example – by being a good communicator yourself. The second step is to set a policy which will draw attention to good communications. The third is to back up your policy with an efficient management reporting system. 15

The public sector is controlled by the government which means their funding is dependent on government allowances. As public sector businesses are not for profit, they don't have as much disposable income to bump up wages at a whim. Typically, public sector workers will be employed on pay grades and they will need to work through the different grades to get a pay increase. A good example of this is the NHS pay band system – the higher the band, the higher the pay, but it takes a while to move through bands. In specific roles like administration, there is only so far you can go meaning pay may become stagnant at some point. These goals may be influenced in some degree by a formal, systematic approach, such as job descriptions and organizational charts. However, most of the activities of a dynamic public sector organization cannot be programmed or even anticipated. By selecting and achieving priorities, more important tasks should be scheduled before other tasks in the administrative process. On the basis of this information, knowledge can be brought to bear upon change improvement in both public and private sectors.

Kenneth Gangel notes:

> First you study the work to be done, the functions, the long-range goals, and then draw the ideal organizational structure, forgetting personalities. The next step is to take the ideal structure to top management and determine what compromises have to be made – mainly because of personalities. However, the ideal structure is not thrown away when the official chart is published. It is kept and continually updated so the future planning does not run counter to the ideal structure, compounding mistakes and necessitating further compromises. 16

The key word in all the above items is adequate. We may never enjoy all the time, money, staff, equipment, and resources we would like to have, but that's not the point. The question is whether we can do our job to a point at which we feel confident we are doing it well. Or we motivate actually on one of benefit, though, is that public sector employees tend to be offered more comprehensive pay packages and benefits, though this can be mirrored in the private sector. In the public sector, whilst there will be budget constraints, there is far more opportunity to grow profits and have out of cycle pay rises throughout the year. In this sector, businesses set their own salaries. Private companies can use Pay data's salary benchmarking service to see what employees across the sector are being paid and what they should be looking to pay their employees.

Whilst the pay might differ, the public sector can offer more job stability. There will always be a need for public sector services such as healthcare, local authorities and law enforcement, meaning those employed in the public sector typically aren't affected by the threat of redundancy or going under due to financial losses. By remembering, we can't reorganize our time for the future until we know how we currently use it. Unless we write achievable, realistic goals and identify how they fit the overall mission, time wasting will become a regular hobby. In contrast, the private sector can be slightly more volatile in terms of job stability, although there are usually more progression opportunities and chances for promotion within one company. When we study, try to think in advance of all the possible ways that we can put what we learn into practice in our public, private and voluntary sectors. For me it is simple – pulpit, radio, manuscript or the social media. You identify your own outlets.

The Voluntary Sector Organisation

The 'voluntary sector' refers to organisations whose primary purpose is to create social impact rather than profit. It is often called the third sector, civil society or the not-for-profit sector. The aim of voluntary organisations is to fulfil their mission and work towards the greater good in some specific way, rather than to make a profit. This often means they prioritise things differently than a business would do. Like the private and statutory sectors, the voluntary sector covers a vast range of activities from the social and cultural to the environmental and political. By far the largest grouping of voluntary activities encompasses health and social welfare. It is within this field of activity that the earliest references to geographies of voluntary activity can be found.

Woodrow Wilson once said that:

> Now at the end of the twentieth century, leadership experts again emphasize this team orientation in leadership. Leadership is now understood by many to imply collective action, orchestrated in such a way as to bring about significant change while raising the competencies and motivation of all those involved – that is, action where more than one individual influence the process. [17]

The attitudes and opinions of people are of great significance, particularly in voluntary organisation sector. But when anticipated attitudes or opinions impede effective decision making, they must be brought into proper perspective. Keep in mind that we seek to build an environment that frees the depths of creativity in the human mind in order that through the wisdom for fresh ideas. Such a global or holistic interest in the voluntary sector, particularly since the 1980s, has generated a variety much debate. However, while many attempts have been made to refine these definitions, at its broadest level it is widely accepted that it refers to that sector of society, which encompasses formal, non-profit distributing organizations that are both self-governing and constitutionally independent of the state.

Though voluntary organizations may employ paid staff and receive funding from the state, their remit is to act for public rather than shareholder benefit. Again Terry Edwards, mention:

> The next fundamental principle that pervaded the church voluntary sector and continued on and on was the spirit of caring and compassionate equality. To make sure no one was in need of food or shelter, those that had extra land and real estate (ktemata) and extra personal property (hyparxis) sold them and turned the money in to the church (voluntary sector) for distribution. I don't think the text implics that they sold their immediate homes. This was not communal living, nor was it communism; it was a caring community. [18]

The voluntary sector is independent from local and national government, and distinct from the private sector. Charities are the largest single category within the voluntary sector. Others include community benefit societies and co-operatives, not-for-profit community businesses or community interest companies (CICs), credit unions and small informal community groups. Voluntary organisations often need to balance the competing interests of a wide range of stakeholders and will put a premium on ensuring all stakeholders, including staff and volunteers, are in agreement with its goals and plans. This will involve discussion and consideration by large numbers of people with differing viewpoints. Voluntary organisations do not normally have large budgets, and the budgets they do have are rarely flexible. People who donate to charity rightly expect their money to be spent carefully and as originally stated. Voluntary organisations therefore need to be creative and do more with less. Volunteers, skills based and otherwise, often play a role in voluntary organisations. Thirty one percent of the public say that they have benefited from or used services from a charity (Charity Commission Research 2017 in UK).

In a serious work like this, we must walk a tight line between becoming too technical and yet avoiding essential distinctions. Consequently, it seems useful at this point that voluntary organisation achieve their aims through a wide range of activities, such as providing services or other forms of direct support and advice to the groups they help; for example, running a women's shelter or providing legal advice. Some also aim to achieve long-term or systemic change. They may work at a local or national level, or globally. Things may move more slowly in the voluntary sector than elsewhere. This is because there is an emphasis on collaboration and consensus (see above).

Additionally, limited and ring-fenced budgets mean finding resources for new projects takes more time and ingenuity. Voluntary sector organisations exist to fulfil a specific social purpose, whereas the primary goal of private sector organisations is to make a profit for shareholders. Some aspects of the way they work can appear similar to other sectors, but there are a few cultural differences which may surprise first-time volunteers.

Most important to the user is the task to be achieved, how success will be evaluated, the knowledge and resources necessary to complete it, and a confidence in their fitness for purpose. While the records requirement is to capture evidence into a repository that accurately reflects past events, the user requirement is for evidence that guides choice between possible forward actions. Whether this evidence stems from personal experience or is acquired from an external source, the kinds of question that the business user asks of this knowledge are: Will it help to produce the right result? Is it from a trustworthy source? Is it biased or slanted? Will it work for me in these circumstances? Is it practical and actionable?

Outcomes are broader based and assessed at a collective level, as an aggregation of individual cases, and at a systemic level, where the value of the whole is greater than the sum of the parts. They are more intangible, harder to define, measure and produce, and are bound up with ideas and values: whether an outcome is considered desirable is contentious, its effects are contestable and its priority subject to change. Example outcomes include: low unemployment and fast return to work; patient lifestyle changes resulting in reduced hospital admissions; reduction in child abuse through improved parenting skills.

Finally, it is important to acknowledge that this particular configuration of civil society with the urban lab model of smart city development engaged in by the local council places another parameter on engagement in smart city activity in Jamaica, United State or United Kingdom etc. These conflicts of purpose and interest are perhaps less visible in a smart city like Jamaica, United State or United Kingdom etc which different projects appear and disappear generally rather quickly, very often dependent on short-lived funding or goodwill. They may be more evident—and challenging—in a smart city with a more centralized and strategic approach to smart city activity.

Chapter Two
Operating Model for Organisational Theory and Design

Organisation Design Definition

Many of the studies of "operating model for organizational theory and design" have been influenced by the priorities of management. They have been concerned with how to make organizations including the church more efficient and in particular how to improve the productivity of workers. There were few systematic training programmers to teach workers their jobs and often skills were acquired simply by watching more experienced colleagues. Once management has developed a science for each element of a man's work, it must then select and train workers in the new methods. Workers and tasks must be closely matched.

According to Taylor:

> There is one best way of performing any work task. It is the job of management to discover this way by applying scientific principles to the design of work procedures. For example, various tools should be tested to find the most efficient for the job; rest periods of differing length and frequency should be tried to discover the relationship between rest and

productivity; and the various movements involved in the task should be assessed in order to find those that are least time consuming and produce the lowest level of fatigue. [19]

With this approach, Taylor laid the foundation for what has come to be known as time and motion studies. Thus, in order to maximize productivity and obtain work of the highest quality, the manager must give some special incentive to his workers beyond that which is given to the average in the trade. In practice this identifies that, different organizational structures and processes are needed for effectiveness in different situations. Some major elements affecting the choice of structures are the organization's strategy, its technology, its size and even the preferences of its top managers. Environments differ also, and what is suitable in organizational design in one environment may not be suitable in another. Since environments change over time (sometimes rapidly), there is a special need for organizational designs to be adaptable so that they can be changed to best fit the changing environment. The contingency point of view requires a significant change in philosophy from the traditional view that, there are preferred ways of organizing that could remain relatively fixed over time.

According to Lewicki, Barry and Saunders:

> Organisational theory and design defined power as the ability of an individual to bring about outcomes in which that person desires or in other words, having the ability to get things done exactly how they want. It is however important to note that power does not

reside from within the individual but is rather determined by the individual's relationship to his or her environment. In 1959, social psychologists John French and Bertram Raven identified five sources of power, as they were in the belief that the processes of power are rather pervasive, complex, and most times a disguise in society. These sources of power stems from reward power, coercive power, legitimate power, referent power, and expert power. [20]

If tasks are constant and well defined, varying very little from month to month and year to year, a mechanistic form tends to be superior. If changes in the technology, market and other parts of the environment are minimal, then a mechanistic structure seems to be more efficient. Worker attitude also are a contingency factor. If workers like more routine tasks and direction from others, then a mechanistic form better meets their needs. If they are threatened by uncertainty and insecurity, then a mechanistic approach is better. Ideologically, it legitimates the idea of a fair day's pay for a fair day's work. Furthermore, it easier to control and regulate the skilled worker and the increasing division of labour makes it difficult for even the most skilled workers to understand the whole production process.

Organic forms are more efficient in other situations and these situations tend to be more archetypal in modem society. Organic forms work better if the environment is dynamic, requiring frequent changes within the organization. They also work better when the tasks are not defined well enough to become routine. If employees seek autonomy, openness, variety, change and chances to try new approaches, then an organic form is better. If they do not, a mechanistic form may still be preferred. Teams are more likely to be utilized within an organic form of organization, because they provide the flexibility that modern organizations require.

The Reward Power, according to the results from the ability to provide positive reinforcement for a desired behaviour which some scholars believed that this power depends on one's ability to administer the positive valences in order to eliminate the negative valences. This power was also dependent upon the probability that an individual can mediate the reward that is perceived by another. When individuals are of the knowledge that they will be rewarded upon carrying out a desired task, the probability is high for them to complete the task. Yet despite the autonomy given to highly qualified employees, management is still in control because they decide which professionals to recruit and which departments to expand or contract.

For example, if the manager of stock exchange gives out a task to be completed within a maximum of two weeks, while also stating that the first individual to complete the task of selling 20 different stocks will be compensated by way of a tangible or intangible compensation, then individuals will feel more motivated to carry out the task. This gives the manager the power over the employees, having to possess a resource in which can be rewarded to the workers. However, it is important to note that if the reward does not have much perceived value to the workers, the power over the employees weakens.

According to Lunenburg:

> An organization is considered mechanistic when it is characterized by a rigid hierarchy, high levels of formalization, a heavy reliance on rules, vertical specialization, centralized decision making, and narrowly defined tasks. In contrast, an organization is considered organic when it characterized by a weak or multiple hierarchies, low level of formalization, horizontal specialization, decentralized decision making, and the fluidity of tasks. [21]

<u>Coercive Power</u>, with the belief that it was rather similar with reward power where it involves the ability of an individual to manipulate the attainment of valences. A contingency approach to organizing may be useful within an organization, with the result that various departments may be organized differently to meet their particular needs. The research department may have an organic structure and the production department may demand a mechanistic structure. However, with the view that coercive power reflected potential to inflict punishment and as such, these two types of power were quite the opposite of each other though both are dependent upon the ability of the inferior individuals to carry out the required course of action. Peter Blau wrote:

> The higher the level of qualifications of the staff, the more authority and decision making was decentralized. When responsibility is delegated, a high ratio of managers is

> required, not for supervision and direction but
> for communication and consultation. Since an
> expert staff can make greater contributions to
> operating procedures, there is a greater need
> to ensure that information flows upwards
> from the lower ranks. [22]

But we made it clear that the strength of the coercive power lies within the magnitude of the negative valences of the threatened punishments given by the superior, multiplied by the perceived probability which the inferior conforms to. For example, the CEO of Stock Exchange is superior to all employees, whether some employees are in position of a supervisor or head of a department. These managers tend to imply or threaten employees of being demoted, denied privileges, or even to be fired to bring their point across and show superiority. This behaviour could also result from the manager simply wanting to get a task completed in a limited amount of time. However, this does not justify a good enough reason for this behaviour, and as such can lead to dissatisfaction in the workplace due to abuse of power.

When division of work and delegation are planned correctly, the result is a complex web of relationships that links people into efficient working organization. Each level has functional teams that are linked to the next level above and below them. This is known as linking pin concept. Each manager serves as a linking pin connecting that manager's group with the rest of the organization. If all linking pins are effective, then the organization can function as an integrated whole. Conversely, if there is a weakness anywhere in the chain of linking pins, the organization will be inclined to be less effective. When managers see themselves as linking pins uniting and catering to the whole organization, they operate more effectively. Maintaining such an organization-wide perspective can be problematic, especially when managers are held responsible for their own unit's results and are compensated on the basis of its performance. Nonetheless, when employees understand a manager's role as a linking pin for the whole organization the managers can serve to both their unit and the organization as a whole more effectively.

<u>The Legitimate Power,</u> declaring that such power is based upon authority recognized within society based on the position obtained within an organizational structure. One study of claims adjusters and their supervisors in an insurance company indicated that, several factors it seems that contributed to a higher degree of delegation. Among them were the supervisor's perception of subordinates as able and trustworthy and the presence of a heavy work load on the supervisor. Delegation of authority is also possible when supervisors believe that employees hold the necessary background information to make a wise decision and when the outcome of an employee's decision would create only minimal risk for the organization. Management is always looking for increasing the organizational performance and for that purpose they make heavy use of teams. Effective teams have definitely certain common characteristics and forming a team doesn't always increase its performance.

Laurie Mullins wrote:

> The art of delegation is to agree clear terms of reference with subordinates, to give them the necessary authority and responsibility and then

to monitor their performance without undue interference or the continual checking of their work. Effective delegation provides a means of social skills. It requires a clear understanding of people perception, reliance on other people, confidence and trust, and courage. It is important that the manager choose the right subordinates to whom to delegate authority and responsibility. The manager must know what to delegate, when and to whom. [23]

In rare cases however, employees will still abide by a demand by a demoted supervisor out of respect and the impact the person has created while in such position. There are many types of teams created by different types of organization. These creations are after identifying common types of terms usually noticed in the present managerial organizations.

Referent Power according to the function of the respect and esteem accorded to an individual by virtue of personal attributes, to which others identify. In other words, this team often outperform individuals when dealing with tasks involving multiple skills, precise judgment and dependable experience. Many successful organizations have structured themselves to compete effectively and efficiently by turning to formation of teams as a technique to use the employee's talents in a better manner. By the way, teams are said to be more adaptable and reacting to changing events than the usual departments of an organization. Classical organization theory is the process of commencing with the total amount of work to be done and dividing it into divisions, departments, jobs and assignments of responsibilities to people. It is accomplished by means of division of work creating levels of authority and functional units and delegation allocating duties, authority and responsibility to others.

The result is an operating hierarchy, which is visually highlighted in an organization chart. Each organization structures itself and operates somewhat differently. This means that an individual would have the knowledge and skills to evaluate a given situation while effectively providing suggestions and making recommendations for solutions. This can be demonstrated in the workplace where an issue arises, for example the computer systems have been hacked in and it requires extra computer knowledge and skills to fix the problem. An individual with such a skill, being able to counteract this situation while making recommendations and giving high tech solutions will allow them obtain a level of leadership in such subject area.

The Importance of Organisation Structure
The purpose of structure is the division of work among members of the organisation, and the coordination of their activities so they are directed towards the goals and objectives of the organisation. Structure is the pattern of relationships among positions in the organisation and among members of the organisation. Structure makes possible the application of the process of management and creates a framework of order and command through which the activities of the organisation can be planned, organised, directed and controlled.

Structure is clearly importance for any organisation, whatever its size. However, in the smaller organisations there are likely to be fewer problems of structure. The distribution of tasks, the definition of authority and responsibility, and the relationship between members of the organisation can be established on a personal and informal basis. With increasing size, however, there is greater need for a carefully designed and purposeful form of organisation. There is need for a formal organisational structure. There is also need for a continual review of structure to ensure that it is the most appropriate form for the particular organisation, and in keeping with its growth and development.

According to Drucker:

> It is the correct design of structure which is of most significance in determining organisational performance. Good organisation structure does not by itself produce good performance. But a poor organisation structure makes good performance impossible, no matter how good the individual managers may be. To improve organisation structure...will therefore always improves performance. [24]

The managerial situation is one of objective facts and events but the duty of the manager is to impose a subjective judgement to try to isolate reasons for these events or to try to impose a direction on future action. The structure of an organisation affects not only productivity and economic efficiency but also the morale and job satisfaction of the workforce. Getting the structure right is the first step in organisational change. Structure should be designed, therefore, so as to encourage the willing participation of members of the organisation and effective organisational performance.

It must be realised that these judgements are subjective in nature and, as such, prone to potential error. The skilled manager should be aware of these subjective features of judgements and should ensure that the subjective element has not caused him, her to misjudge the situation faced.

According to Dr. Needle, words:

> At the strategic level we are concerned with those management decisions, and the influences on those decisions which determine the direction of business activities. Strategic decisions will influence such factors as the product range, the amount spent on advertising, the recognition of trade unions and so on. The managing director of a small firm with a potentially profitable innovation often faces a strategic dilemma. Alternatives might be to sell the idea for development by a larger firm or simply accept a merger with the larger organization; both of which may be personally unacceptable to the owner of the small business. [25]

The functions of the formal structure, and the activities and defined relationships within it, exist independently of the members of the organisation who carry out the work. In practice, the actual operation of the organisation and success in meeting its objectives will depend upon the behaviour of people who work within the structure and who give shape and personality to the framework.

The objectives of this chapter are to:
1. Give some insight into the consultancy process.
2. Introduce 'how decisions happen' in organisations.

3. Gain some understanding of the skills used in undertaking decision making.
4. Give some experience of using those skills.

This is illustrated by the manager who identifies poor performance from an employee – once this poor performance has been identified it will require great effort on the part of the employee to convince the manger that he or she has changed. It must be stated that the manager's judgement is not totally affected by the halo effect – that is excellent performance should be detected readily. The problem is that significant, but not startling, improvements in performance may not be detected easily or will not be detected immediately by the manager.

R. Stewart, for example, found the relationship between people and organisation to be reciprocal.

> People modify the working of the formal organisation, but their behaviour is also influenced by it. It may make demands on them which they find an undue strain, so that they seek ways of modifying these pressures. The method of work organisation can determine how people relate to one another, which may affect both their productivity and their morale. Managers, therefore, need to be conscious of the ways in which methods of work organisation may influence people's attitudes and actions. Before behaviour is put down to individual or group cussedness, managers should look for its possible organisational causes. [26]

Building an organisation involves more than concern for structure, methods of work and technical efficiency. The hallmark of many successful business organisations is the attention given to the human element; to the development of a culture which helps to create a feeling of belonging, commitment and satisfaction. Structure must be designed, therefore, so as to maintain the balance of the socio-technical system and the effectiveness of the organisation as a whole. My attention must be given to the interactions between both the structural and technological requirements of my religious organisation; and social factors and the needs and demands of the human part of the organisation. The organisation is structured into four regions: North; South; East and West. Each region has a director who has an input into organisational policy and has full accountability for his or her region. Each region is made up of approximately four areas, each holding several headed. We seem surprised and disappointed when others do not respond as enthusiastically as we expect.

Again it must be stressed that this is not simple issue; rather each manager is capable of understanding both points of view but they enter the managerial situation with different priorities. The determination of policy and decision-making, the execution of work, and the exercise of authority and responsibility are carried out by different people at varying levels of seniority throughout the organisation structure. Being the Managing Director I need to produce a short proposal outlining how my consultancy will tackle an equal opportunities audit. I do not spend too much time considering the financial constraints, although, obviously, a consideration of resources is necessary so that my proposal is realistic.

My proposal, have, include:

a. Methodology: What research methods will you use to get the necessary information? Where will you look for the information, for example with which groups of people, which documents and so on?
b. Production: The new site operating under the latest technology offers management a speedier and more flexible operation with a capability of increased capacity.
c. Marketing: In marketing terms, the case illustrates how the need for change has arisen through increased competition and reduced barriers to entry for would-be competitors.
d. Accounting: The cost of setting up a new operating plant and its commissioning with state –of – the – art technology represents a considerable short-term or long- term investment with a potential for longer term cost saving.

The development of systems thinking from an organisational perspective starts with the analogy of the firm as a living organism. To be effective, the firm, like the organism, must adapt to its environment in order to survive. The inputs, processes and outputs must be balanced so that the firm can obtain equilibrium, especially with its environment. The application of the systems approach in organizational analysis first gained prominence through the utilization of a socio- technical systems perspective. This is based on the assumption that the social system of the firm and its technical system interact in a complex way.

When managers examine a managerial problem they are capable of making mistakes. Some of the mistakes they might make are caused by these perceptual errors. Thus it is essential that the manager is aware of the possibility of making such mistakes. For me to obtain the information for decision making about make this individual person to work one more day a week, I need to find reliable and appropriate sources of information and select methods for gathering that information which are efficient and effective for me. This is about making my significant contributions to improving the team and the organizational performance. Making the improvements covers my own area of responsibility as well as making recommendations for improvements to organizational plans.

1. I have been allocating work to others
2. I have been achieving specific results by using my resources effectively
3. I have been carrying out the organizational policy in my defined area of authority
4. I have been controlling limited financial budgets, and
5. I have been contributing to broader activities such as change programmers and recruitment.

L. J. Mullins wrote this statement on community level:

> In turn, the managerial level interrelates with the community level or institutional level, concerned with broad objectives and the work of the organisation as a whole. Decisions at the community level will be concerned with the selection of operations, and the development of the organisation in relation to external agencies and the wider social environment. Control at the institutional level of the

organisation may be exercised, for example, by legislation, codes of standards or good practice, trade or professional associations, political or governmental action, and public interest. 27

This information which I need to obtain which will be accurate and relevant, and the ways I will deal with insufficient, contradictory or ambiguous information. Organisations have different purposes, different values and different cultures. Where organisations place a high value on people in decisions to ensure that these decisions are effective and implement able. They assume that being decisive means making quick decisions by, themselves, whereas it means making decisions at the right time and in the right way.

In practice, there is not a clear division between determination of policy and decision-making, coordination of activities and the actual execution of work. Most decisions are taken with reference to the execution of wider decisions, and most execution of work involves decision. Therefore, if the organisation as a whole is to perform effectively there must be clear objectives; a soundly designed structure; and good communications, both upwards and downwards, among the different levels of the organisation. The types of qualitative and quantities information which are essential to my role and responsibilities, and how I identify these thought the ranges of sources of information which are available to me.

My invitation to tender (teams):

Mount Educational Board

September

Dear

Further to our recent telephone conversation, I would like to formally invite you to tender for the proposed Equal Opportunities audit. We have identified four key questions which we need to address.

1. How much have we achieved so far?
2. How fair are our existing systems and procedures?
3. How effective are our monitoring systems?
4. What must we do next?

Our focus in the past has been consistent with a traditional equal opportunity approach however we are keen to broaden this to a managing diversity approach.

We need to receive the proposal by 15 September, and we will make our decision by 22 September.

The project must be completed by 15 January next year.

Yours sincerely

Allan P. Miller
Human Resources

To improve work activities, I need to monitor activities, trends and developments and invite others to come forward with their suggestions for improvements. If conduct does not improve, the charge may result in dismissal. You need to plan the change, check people's understanding and commitment to the change and monitor the implementation of your plans to ensure the intended improvements are achieved. I also need to ensure that work quality is maintained to an acceptable standard during the period of change.

1. I ensure that I identify the information I need to make the required decisions. And the sources of information are reliable and sufficiently wide-ranging to meet current and likely future information requirements.
2. I will mail a personal letter to team and senior manager, about provide information for a decision to make.
3. I am informing these individuals of a time and place for this meeting on the decision for individual's person to work one more a day a week.
4. My methods of obtaining information are consistent with organizational values, policies and legal requirements.
5. Where I find information is inadequate, contradictory or ambiguous, I take prompt and effective action to deal with this error.

It is a help here, obviously when it comes to building up and maintaining the team or meeting individual needs everyone should pitch in – there is just too much to be done for any one person to do it all himself or herself. That is also true, of course, in all the task circle. But there is one general function or activity that stands out and needs to be looked at closely – decision making. How far should the leader make or take the decisions him or her? Would you accept that as the key issue?

Dr. John Adair wrote:

> Yes, the more freedom you give people in a decision, the less you are in direct control of the outcome. That's why managers sometimes find it very hard to delegate when they should be doing so. But there's much to be said for making decisions as high up the continuum as possible. For the more that the team – or an individual colleague, if you are working on a one-to –one basis – shares in a decision, the greater will be their motivation to implement it. [28]

I believe what Dr. Adair is saying that, 'the actual process itself – providing you are honest and open about it – is not manipulative'. I know all about it, and yet it's true for us that if your managers take the time and make the effort to involve us in the decision – making process, we are far more likely to feel committed and give our best when it comes to making it happen.

The Importance of the Hierarchy

We have referred previously to the significance of the changing nature of the work organisation. However, the increasing use of group or team approaches, the growth of flexible employment, increasing use of sub-contracting, an emphasis on participation and empowerment, and many workers involved in decision-making have all led to changes in the traditional boos- subordinate relationship. This has led to a discussion on the role of the hierarchy in modern organisations and the extent to which managers can rely solely on their perceived formal authority within the structure of the organisation.

Communication can take many forms and embrace a variety of media. But treating someone as an equal does not mean they are equal. The variety of media will be presented in a form which shows the various alternatives available to the manager in the choice of mode of delivery. This helps managers to assess their personal qualities and consider what motivates and satisfies them at work, giving them the opportunity to identify different career options and ways of developing their careers within an organisation, and allowing them to begin the process of matching themselves to possible career options. However informal the environment, you can't escape from a functional hierarchy although the more skilled the company's work, the fewer tiers of management and the fewer individual managers should be required. For me to make this statement to all the team members whose understanding and commitment by confirm by provision of appropriate information identify the trends.

According to Tony Dawson:

> It is often assumed that communication takes the form of telling someone to do something. However communication is a much more extended, complex and subtle process, embracing careful examination of what is to be transmitted, how it is to be transmitted, ensuring the existence of an environment conducive to full understanding of the message sent, ensuring that the message received has been identical to that sent, and finally that the

communication has been accepted and acted upon by its recipient. [29]

Traditionally, senior managers have been concerned with setting the strategic direction and objectives for the organisation; middle managers with making it happen – resource and managing the changes. The corollary is that senior managers are concerned with results and middle managers with how these are achieved. Has a manager I have to analyze every, information to support this decision making to achieve these objectives and goals. I select what I identify and was supported by good evidence, which emerge from the information with conclusions that this individual can work one more day a week. With the internal and external trends which have a bearing on the future improvements, including any changes in legislation or national service standards.

1. I make it clear the differences between fact and opinion, and how to identify these accordingly.
2. My leadership style has develops and help me to present a reasoned case based on the outcomes of my analysis the need.
3. I research the advice and information I needs of the individual in ways which are appropriate and sufficient and takes account of my organizational constraints.
4. I may it I responsibilities the advice is consistent with the organizational policy, procedures, constraints and legal requirements.
5. I advise all the team supported by reasoned argument and appropriate evidence.

There is a lot of muddled thinking about hierarchies and the whole issue of how equally we treat people within companies. Reinforces the authority of individual decisions – when a decision of significant importance has to be taken there is a tendency for individuals to be fearful of making such a decision or feel the need for collective ratification of such a decision. Under such circumstances the formation of a committee will help the various members to afford to each other mutual support. However informal the environment, you can't escape from a functional hierarchy although the more skilled the company's work, the fewer tiers of management and the fewer individual managers should be required. The precise nature of career management will vary for different people, depending upon their current work situation and the extent to which, and the ways in which, they want it to develop. Thus individuals will find different exercises relevant at different times in their working lives.

It is important to bear in mind that there are many variables which influence the most appropriate organisation structure and system of management, including situational factors and the contingency approach. Changing patterns of work organisation, the demand for greater flexibility and the multi-skills challenge, and managerial processes such as delegation and empowerment also have a major interrelationship with structure and influence decisions on structural design. It takes the organizational values and policies and the legal requirements which I have a bearing on the collection of information and how I interpret these information. One need to check the recipients' understanding of the information and advice you have provided and observe rules and guidelines on confidentiality, and the law on data protection. By reading and studying Dr. Sally

Maitlis, five key steps of career management and offers a number of exercises that explore them.

Dr. Sally Maitlis wrote:

1. Self- assessment – identifying your values, skills, and interests.
2. Exploring career options – identifying opportunities within and without the organisation.
3. Matching yourself to opportunities – determining the fit between yourself and different options. Decision making and goal setting – choosing a preferred route, setting realistic targets and action plans.
4. Follow – up – ongoing monitoring and review. 30

It has become clear that organisation is not an absolute. It is a tool for making people productive in working together. While recognising that there is clearly no one right organisation, there is nevertheless in the final analysis, an underlying need to establish a framework of order and system of command by which the work to be undertaken is accomplished successfully. This demands that attention be given to certain basic principles and considerations in the design of organisation structure, or in reviewing the effectiveness of an existing structure. We have come now to the highest level of leadership in corporate enterprise. Establishing what you have to give to a job and what you want from work are important starting points in management. Once you are clear about yourself and your needs, it becomes possible to start evaluating the suitability of different career options. In other words, it's the thinking and planning appropriate to a military general or, by analogy, to the leader of any large organisation.

I shall try to see the present position clearly and realistically. That means asking myself; "What are we actually doing now? What do we do well? What are our strengths and weakness?" It may not be easy to find the answers to these questions, but they strike me as essential.

1. I ensure that all given opportunities to make recommendations for the work activities improvements.
2. I ensure that monitoring the activities occurs at intervals most likely to identify potential improvements.
3. I ensure the information I gather on trends and developments is relevant, reliable and sufficient to identify potential improvements.
4. I ensure the team that present my plans for implementing change to clients at an appropriate time, level and pace.
5. I ensure confirm with the team members understanding of the implications of the change and their commitment to their role in it, including identifying any resistance to the change.

According to O. Lundy and A. Cowling:

> Organisations are collections of people brought together for a purpose. To achieve this purpose successfully, people need to be organised within the best possible structure.

> Decisions on structure are primary strategic decisions. Structure can make or break an organisation. [31]

Different management approaches will be more or less appropriate for people at different stages of their working lives. When considering a new job or new organisation, it can be hard to know just what you are looking for and whether it will be as good as or better than your current one. The nature of the organisation and its strategy will indicate the most appropriate organisational levels for different functions and activities, and the formal relationships between them. Clearly defined objectives will help facilitate systems of communication between different parts of the organisation and the extent of decentralisation and delegation. Some clues to what motivates you at work can be found by reviewing past work experiences, identifying what it was that made them positive or negative.

People considering future career options are often surprisingly unaware of the skills and personal attributes they have to offer. Knowing these can help you to identify jobs in which you are most likely to be successful, and it can also assist you in getting them. While it is not always possible to fit a job directly to your interests, you are more likely to enjoy and find satisfying work that to some extent matches them. These are the basic activities of the organisation which are related to the actual completion of the productive process and directed towards specific and definable end-results. To ensure the efficient achievement of overall objectives of the organisation, the results of the task functions must be coordinated.

Strategic Management Process on the Current State

Strategic management is a particular course of action that is meant to achieve a corporate goal in organisational like the colleges and universities. Management deals with the process that drives the organization towards its performance. This means that our colleges or universities have an office of student affairs. This basis on which jobs are grouped together is called departmentalization. Once each of the college organizations has its own specific way of classifying and grouping work activities, great results can be achieved. This approach can be used in all types of organizations, although the functions change to reflect the organization's purpose and work. Product departmentalization groups jobs by product line. In this approach, each major product area is placed under the authority of a manager who is responsible for everything having to do with that product line.

As R. Stewart has pointed out manager who think about what can be done only in terms of what they can do, cannot be effective. He wrote:

> Managers must learn to accept their dependence upon people. A key part of being a good manager is managing that dependence. Managers who say that they cannot delegate because of poor staff may genuinely be unfortunate in the caliber of the staff that they have inherited or been given. More often this view is a criticism of themselves: a criticism either of their unwillingness to delegate when they could and should do so, or a criticism of their selection, training and development of their staff. [32]

In this approach, work activities follow a natural processing flow of products or even of customers. The processes which are to be followed to initiate the colleges or university's organizational structure and to create strategies and the steps to be taken by managers are all about management. The Strategic Management Process defines the goals and objectives for a business, it creates the action plan so that a company can reach them and then it follows the plan. For example, organisations like Miller's Bible College and Institution organizes each of its divisions along functional lines: its manufacturing units around processes, its sales units around numbers of college's geographic regions, and its sales regions into five customer groupings. There five steps in Strategic Management Process which colleges and universities managers need to follow; which are defined as under:

1. Identify the Current Mission, Objectives, and Strategies: It is important to identify the goals and objectives of the company. It defines the present purpose of the organization as a mission and the strategies currently being followed. The mission statement becomes the identification of an organization so it is very much necessary to identify it. Making the chain of command is the continuous line of authority that extends from upper organizational levels to the lowest levels and clarifies who reports to whom. It helps employees answer questions such as "Who do I go to if I have a problem?" or "To whom am I responsible?" You cannot discuss the chain of command without discussing these other concepts: authority, responsibility, accountability, unity of command, and delegation. Authority refers to the rights inherent in a managerial position to tell people what to do and to expect them to do it.

Making work specialization describes to which the overall task of the organization is broken down and divided into smaller component parts. For example, one person would paint a wall and another person fixes a door. So, by breaking jobs up into small tasks, it could be performed over and over every 10 seconds while using employees (like the students) who had relatively limited skills. Examples to facilitate decision making and coordination, an organization's managers are part of the chain of command and are granted a certain degree of authority to meet their responsibilities. As managers coordinate and integrate the work of employees (students), those employees (students) assume an obligation to perform any assigned duties. This obligation or expectation to perform is known as responsibility.

The main thought of this process is that the entire job is not done by an individual and it is broken down into steps, and a different person completes each step. Thus, the work will be done efficiently and effectively. It saves time and also the employee's (student's) skills of performing his job successfully increase through repetition. The responsibility brings with it accountability, which is the need to report and justify work to a (teacher's) manager's superiors. The unity of command principle helps preserve the concept of a continuous line of authority. It states that every employee should receive orders from only one superior. Without unity of command, conflicting demands and priorities from multiple (teachers) managers can create problems. Because (teachers) managers have limited time and knowledge, they may delegate some of their responsibilities to other staffs. Delegation is the assignment of authority to another person to carry out specific duties, allowing the employee to make some of the decisions.

It also has some disadvantages as well. When specialization is overdone, jobs can become more simplified. And when employees do one single task, they become bored and tired. Also, the scope of the employee's growth will be limited. Specialization in one task is good but by getting the training for all other tasks too, is better to cop up with other activities in the company.

2. Analyze the Environment:

It is a process of monitoring the organizational environment to identify competitor's actions and to confirm if it is suitable to let the firm go to already set directions to reach its goals. It can be another element in an organizational design, which is defined an order which authority and power in on college or university organization is used and delegated from top management to the lower management. It also ensures clear assignment of duties and responsibilities of every employee (teacher) at every level.

Instead of information being confined to bosses alone, in addition, information technology has provided employees with immediate access to information instead of waiting to hear from someone higher up in the chain of command. Line managers are responsible for the essential activities of the colleges or university organizations, including matriculation of new students and graduation processes. College and university line managers have the authority to issue orders to those in the chain of command. The president, the production manager, and the sales manager are examples of line managers. Staff managers work in the supporting activities of the organizations, such as human resources or accounting. Staff managers have advisory authority and cannot issue orders to those in the chain of command (except those in their own department).

Assume that we have four college or university organizations, each of them having sixty four employees; one of college or university organization has a uniform span of five levels on span of eighteen subjects. If the average saves £250 000 a year, the other colleges or university organizations with the same wider span would save more than £600 000 each a year in management salaries alone. However, at some point, the others wider spans in thinking of effectiveness. When the span becomes large, there will be improvement in employees' performance times to provide the necessary leadership and support.

3. Analyze the Organization's Resources:

By analyzing the college's or university organization's resources, an institution can make a pictorial view of the available capabilities and resources inside and outside of the organization. It will help to determine the college or university organization's competitive weapons, that is, value creating skills, capabilities and resources. This way, the span of control in an organization is defined as the number of employees reporting directly to one supervisor / manager. It is said, the wider the span, the more efficient the organization. It determines the number of employees that a manager can effectively and efficiently manage.

In the modern world, the contemporary view of span of control recognizes that many factors influence the appropriate number of employees a manager can efficiently and effectively manage. These factors include the skills and abilities of the manager and the employees, and the characteristics of the work being done. For example, the more training and experience employees have the less direct supervision they need. Therefore, managers with well-trained and experienced employees can function quite well with a wider span. Other contingency variables that determine the appropriate span include similarity of employee tasks, the complexity of those tasks, the physical proximity of subordinates, the degree to which standardized procedures are in place and the sophistication of the organization's information system.

4. Identify Strengths and Weaknesses:

Formalization refers to the degree to which jobs within the college or university organization are standardized and the extent to which employee's behaviour is guided by rules and procedures. If a job is highly formalized, the person doing that job has little freedom to choose what is to be done, when it is to be done, and how he or she does it. Employees can be expected to handle the same input in exactly the same way, resulting in consistent and uniform output. College or university organizations with high formalization have explicit job descriptions, numerous organizational rules, and clearly defined procedures covering work processes. On the other hand, where formalization is low, job behaviours are relatively unstructured, and employees have a great deal of freedom in how they do their work. The degree of formalization varies widely among organizations and even within organizations.

It identifies the strengths and weaknesses within the college or university organization. It also can be defined as SWOT analysis which has the remaining two components, that is, 'strengths' and 'weaknesses'. Strengths are internal activities being done by one colleges or university organization which helps an organization to achieve its goal. And the weaknesses are the activities that are not being done by an organization which is unfavourable for the organization to achieve its goal.

For example, at a newspaper, news reporters often have a great deal of discretion in their jobs. They may pick their news topics, find their own stories, research them the way they want to, and write them up, usually within minimal guidelines. In contrast, employees who lay out the newspaper pages do not have that type of freedom. They have constraints—both time and space—that standardize how they do their work. By reassessing the organization's mission and objectives helps to review the firm's current performance and also to take better actions for the success of the organization. It defined as SMART which means Specific, Measurable, Achievable, Realistic, and Timeframe.

5. Implement Strategies:
Has this employee done something wrong? He did "break" the rule. But by breaking the rule, he actually brought in revenue and provided the customer good service— so good, in fact, that the customer may be satisfied enough to come back in the future. Because such situations where rules may be too restrictive frequently arise, many organizations allow employees some freedom to make decisions they feel are best under the circumstances. It is the process of distributing resources and putting strategies into an action to achieve its goal and objectives.

When the strategies are executed within the organization, it focuses on the process through which strategies are achieved. It controls the process to determine the effectiveness of a strategy. An organization can evaluate results by reviewing the process, adjusting the mission and objectives and strategies, and by initiating the corrective measures. However, this freedom does not mean that all organizational rules are thrown out the window. There will be rules that are important for employees to follow, and these rules should be explained so employees understand the importance of adhering to them. But for other rules, employees may be given some leadership.

Principles of Organisation
Attention was focused on the requirements of the formal organisation and the search for a common set of principles applicable to all circumstances

1. The Principles of the objectives: Every organisation and every part of the organisation must be an expression of the purpose of the undertaking concerned, or it is meaningless and therefore redundant.
2. The principle of specialisation: The activities of every member of any organised group should be confined, as far as possible, to the performance of a single function.
3. The principle of authority: In every organised group the supreme authority must rest somewhere. There should be clear line of authority to every individual in the group.
4. The principle of definition: The content of each position, both the duties involved, the authority and responsibility contemplated and the relationships with other positions should be clearly defined in writing and published to all concerned.

To record and store information one need to select appropriate and efficient methods which comply with the organisation's policies, legal requirements and national service standards. Also need to give your team members the chance to suggest improvements to the way information is recorded and stored, and recommend improvements yourself.

Again Dawson wrote:

> Information technology may result in wider or easier access to confidential or commercially sensitive information. This is of particular importance in the public service. It must not be assumed that wider access to all information is necessarily desirable. Rather such information may contain items of a personal nature which the person would be loath to disclose to too many people – an example would be certain information contained in school records. In such cases the public service organisation may be under a statutory duty to restrict such information to those who have signed legally binding documents to keep such information confidential. Thus widening the access to such records can be seen to be detrimental to the effective management of the organisation. [33]

Many of the principles are bland statements expressed in non-operation terms and give little basis for specific managerial action; they tend to view people as a given rather than as a variable in the system. However, despite such limitations, the principles do provide general guidance on the structuring of organisations and, as such, it is difficult to argue against them.

1. Your systems and procedures for recording and storing information are suitable for the purpose and make efficient use of resources.
2. The way you record and store information complies with organisational policies and legal requirements.
3. The information you record and store is readily accessible in the required format to authorised people only.

The research team has also provided you with details of a method that can be used to examine the problem, a technique known as interaction analysis. The data that the exercise produces can be used to generate a more efficient job design, that is, one that reduces unnecessary information load. The first task is to identify the job and the job holder(s) that should be analysed. In essence, you will require the job holder to record data about all the different types of interaction that are involved in their work at a number of different time points over a number of days. To do this accurately, you will have to attend first to the following:

a. Negotiating the purpose of and use of the data with the individual.
b. Devising a customised form that you can use to record the information that is associated with the interactions.
c. Setting up a method for data collection.

As with any job analysis technique, you must decide on how often you will ask people to record their activity. The recording forms should be designed so that all the necessary information can be recorded and coded quickly. The data may be used to identify highly redundant or irrelevant information, especially if the data are collected across a number of job roles. Each job or role individual analyse is different, so you need to customise your data collection accordingly. There is no one right point or "style" on the decision – making style, I said. 'If you follow a good leader around all day, you find that he or she is making decisions at different points on the scale. In order to achieve the task and to build the team certain key functions have to be performed such as setting objectives, planning, briefing, controlling, and evaluating.

Planning and development, training, inspection and control may suffer in particular, leading to poor job performance. Every person must know his or her position within the structure of the organisation. The very act of organising introduces the concept of the scalar chain. Most organisation charts demonstrate that this principle is used widely as a basis for organisational design. A clear line of authority and responsibility is necessary for the effective operation of the organisation. It seems to be generally accepted, however, that for reasons of morale and to help decision- making and communications there should be as few levels as possible in the scalar chain. There is the danger of adding to the structure in such a way that it results in increased hierarchical authority and control, leads to the risk of empire building and the creation of unnecessary work in justification of the new position. If efforts are made to reduce the number of levels, however, this may bring about an increase in the span of control with the resulting difficulties already discussed.

Effect of a Deficient Organisational Structure

It is not easy to describe, in a positive manner, what constitutes a 'good' or effective organisation structure although, clearly, attention should be given to the design principles discussed above. However, the negative effects of a poorly designed structure can be identified more easily. Because on organisation is like an organism, with a moment of birth, growth through several distinct stages of development, maturation, and finally and end. Of course, there are numerous pathogens that can prove fatal to a company: seismic shifts in markets, myopic strategic vision, hostile takeovers, unforeseen competitive technologies, and the like. If a company has the competencies that flow from self-awareness and self-regulation, motivation and empathy, leadership skills and open communication, it should prove more resilient no matter what the future brings.

Dr. John McLeod wrote:

> It has always been part of the role of a good manager, supervisor or team leader to be able to respond constructively to the emotional and interpersonal difficulties of members of his or her team or department. In recent years, however, an increasing number of organisations have sought to augment the counselling skills of their managers by making professional counselling available to employees. Counselling is a helping process, usually carried out in an individual face-to-

face relationship that has the aim of assisting a person with a problem to make some progress in the direction of resolving that problem. [34]

Handling this information is undertaken with consideration for the rights of the people to know what information is stored and available and the importance of using appropriate communication methods I use. Counselling is a complex skill, it is possible to identify two basic rules that can be used by anyone who wishes to become more effective and sensitive in this area of their work. How I judge the accuracy, relevance, validity and sufficiency of my information required all the support in decision making in the different contexts. The quality of the work for which I am responsible continues to meet the agreed standard throughout the period of change.

1. I will listen and watch the information.
2. I will read the written and spoken questioning
3. I will formal a research conducted personally by myself
4. I will formal a research conducted by the teams

Urwick lays emphasis:

On the technical planning of the organisation and the importance of determining and laying out structure before giving any thought to the individual members of the organisation. And part of the obvious duty of the manager, it is not a substitute for the need for definite planning of the structure. In short, a very large proportion of the friction and confusion in current society, with its manifest consequences in human suffering, may be traced back directly to faulty organisation in the structure sense. ₃₅

Urwick's emphasis on the logical design of organisation structure rather than the development around the personalities of its members is typical of the classical approach to organisation and management. One may be called on to participate in decision making around the type of counselling of 'staff care' package your organisation might use. Given the counselling needs of your organisation, what would be the advantages and disadvantages of each of these models? The statements from team members who were involved in my information gathering activities I record. Then I select appropriate and efficient methods, which comply with my organization's policies, legal requirements and national service standards. I give my team members the chance to suggest improvements to the way information is recorded and stored, and recommend improvements myself. How one identify, the broader implications of change for the work in the organization and its component parts.

1. I try now to ensure that the systems and procedures for recording and storing information are suitable for the purpose and make efficient use of resources.
2. The information I record and store is readily accessible in the required format to authorized people only. On the computer data bases also and the management brochure for backup.
3. I provide opportunities for the team members to make suggest for improvements to systems and procedures. By make recommendations for

improvements to systems and procedures to the relevant people.

4. I make clear the principles of confidentiality – what information should be made available to which individuals.

For example, Child points out that:

> There are a number of problems which so often mark the struggling organisation and which even at the best of times are dangers that have to be looked for. These are low motivation and morale, late and inappropriate decisions, conflict and lack of coordination, rising costs and a generally poor response to new opportunities and external change. Structural deficiencies can play a part in exacerbating all these problems. [36]

Old ways of doing business no longer work; the increasingly intense competitive challenges of the world economy challenge everyone, everywhere, to adapt in order to prosper under new rules. In the old economy, hierarchies pitted labour against management, with workers paid wages depending on their skills, but that is eroding as the rate of change accelerates. Hierarchies are morphing into networks; labour and management are uniting into teams; wages are coming in new mixtures of options, incentives, and ownership; fixed job skills are giving way to lifelong learning as fixed jobs melt into fluid careers. Poor response to new opportunities and external change may result from: failure to establish specialist jobs concerned with forecasting environmental change; failure to give adequate attention to innovation and planning of change as main management activities; inadequate coordination between identification of market changes and research into possible technological solutions. Rising costs may result from: a long hierarchy of authority with a high proportion of senior positions; an excess of administrative work at the expense of productive work; and the presence of some, or all, of the other organisational problems.

In his discussion on the principles of organisation and coordination, Urwick suggests that 'Lack of design is illogical, cruel, wasteful and inefficient.

1. It is illogical because is good social practice, as in good engineering practice, design should come first. No member of the organisation should be appointed to a senior position without identification of the responsibilities and relationships attached to that position and its role within the social pattern of the organisation.
2. It is cruel because it is the individual members of the organisation who suffer most from lack of design.
3. It is wasteful because it jobs are not put together along the lines of functional specialisation then new members of the organisation cannot be training effectively to take over these jobs.
4. It is inefficient because if the organisation is not founded on principles, managers are forced to fall back on personalities. Unless there are clearly established principles, which are understood by everyone in the organisation, managers will start

'playing politics' in matters of promotion and similar issues. [37]

The structure of an organisation is usually depicted in the form of an organisation chart. This will show, at a given moment in time, how work is divided and the grouping together of activities, the levels of authority and formal organisational relationships. The organisation chart provides a pictorial representation of the overall shape and structural framework of an organisation. At the same time, the meltdown of old organisational forms from a hierarchical wiring diagram into the Mandela of a web, along with the ascendance of teamwork, increases the importance of traditional people skills such as building bonds, influence, and collaboration. And as work changes, these human capacities can help us not just compete, but also nurture the capacity for pleasure, even joy, in our work.

While acknowledging that organisation charts have some uses, Townsend likens them to 'rigor mortis' and advises that they should be drawn in pencil.

> Never formalize, print and circulate them. Good organisations are living bodies that grow new muscles to meet challenges. A chart demoralizes people. Nobody thinks of himself as below other people. And in a good company he isn't. Yet on paper there it is…In the best organisations people see themselves working in a circle as if around one table. [38]

In analysing the effectiveness of structure, consideration should be given to both the formal and technological requirements and principles of design; and to social factors, and the needs and demands of the human part of the organisation. Structure should be designed so as to maintain the balance of the socio-technical system, and to encourage the willing participation of members and effective organisational performance. The structure or charts do not describe what really happens in work organisations. In practice, I am referring to the behaviour of individuals, or sections or groups of people, within the organisation. Human behaviour is capricious and prescriptive methods or principles cannot be applied with reliability. Individuals differ and people bring their own perceptions, feelings and attitudes towards the organisation, styles of management and their duties and responsibilities. The behaviour of people cannot be studied in isolation and we need to understand interrelationships with other variables which comprise the total organisation, including the social context of the work organisation and the importance of the informal organisation.

Finally I recommend this improvement to organizational planning team, where the individual at meeting. The behaviour and actions of people at work will also be influenced by a complexity of motivations, needs and expectations. To advise and inform others, I identify the needs to give this individual's one more day a week to work. Structure provides the framework of an organisation and makes possible the application of the process of management. This individual's will then advice on the starting day and time and cost rules and guidelines on confidentiality, and the law on data protection. The structure of an organisation affects not only productivity and economic efficiency but also the morale and job satisfaction of its members.

New Styles of Organisational Design

New styles of organizational design involve shaping company positions and employees into various structures. Many small companies may have little or no structure when starting out. But eventually company management must start forming various departments for greater efficiency and accountability. Any college or university organized design or structure also enhances communication and makes better use of company resources. Small-college or university owners often develop the structures of their organization around company goals, competitors and government regulations. Understanding how different organizational designs work will help you choose the right one for your business.

The Functional Model

A functional structure is one that is centred round basic functions, including accounting, marketing, engineering, finance and human resources. A small company executive may start out hiring managers in each of these functional areas. Managers may, in turn, hire analysts or coordinators under them. And as the companies grow, managers may become directors and vice presidents, overseeing large functional departments. I. Worthington and C. Britton view this as:

> External influences are almost in number
> and variety and no study could hope to
> consider them all. For students of business
> and for managers alike, the requirement is
> to recognize the complexity of the external
> environment and to pay greater the most
> pertinent and pressing for the organization in
> guesting, rather than to adopted to consider all
> people contingencies. 39

The advantage of a functional structure is that it makes efficient use of human resources. Employees in each department specialize or have expertise in one area like marketing. Hence, they work together to synergistically develop the best marketing strategies. A downside to the functional structure is that department goals sometimes take priority over company goals.

Customer Oriented Structure

The objective behind a customer (student) structure is positioning employees (teachers) or department so they can best serve the customers (students). Some small companies (colleges or universities) may sell (teach) to a diverse customer (student) base. This can be especially the case with companies (colleges or universities) which service other business customers (degrees students). The company (college or university) the people perception, both the employees and the organisation can be negatively affected. Time is one of the most valuable, but limited, resources and it is important that the manager utilizes time to the maximum advantage. Making delegation provides a means of training and development, and testing the subordinate's suitability for promotion. It can be used as a means of assessing the likely performance of a subordinate at a higher level of authority and responsibility.

Ulrich suggests that with the changing and dynamic contextual factors:

> The essence of organizations has shifted and will continue to shift from focusing on structure to capability. Capability represents what the organization is able to do and how it

does it rather than the more visible picture of who report to whom and which rules govern work... organizations will operate in the future to identify and nurture a handful of critical capabilities. 40

The concept of delegation provides an opportunity for straightforward practice. But anyone with experience of working situation is likely to be aware of the importance of delegation and the consequences of badly managed delegation. Successful delegation is a social skill. Where managers lack these skills, or do not have a sufficient awareness of the people perception. The selling process may be diverse with each type of customer, requiring special expertise and knowledge. Therefore, departments may need to design their structures around customers to best meet their needs.

Chapter Three

A Configuration Model of Organisational Cultural Theory

The Meaning of Organisation Development

The purpose of this chapter is to give the Miller's Bible College and Institution team the tools for renewal that it needs so that it can continue to grow and be important to the organisation's culture. Being an undergraduate in the past years, and now doing this graduate programme - and hoping to do my doctorate degree later – I have come to believe that the active culture behaviours described in this chapter are valuable in virtually any leader- follower relationship special for example within this Bible College organisation. There are probably specific situations, however, in which the culture behaviours are especially needed and effective.

Organisation development is concerned with the diagnosis of organisational health and performance, and the ability of the organisation to adapt to change. It involves the applications of organisational behaviour and recognition of the social processes of the organisation. In a very general sense, organisation development is concerned with attempts to improve the overall performance and effectiveness of an organisation. Organisation development is a generic term embracing a wide range of intervention strategies into the social processes of an organisation. Theses intervention strategies are aimed at the development of individuals, groups and the organisation as a total system. Large, complex organisations understand that one of the most important duties of the management of their organisation is ensuring that adequate structures and adequate processes exist to properly manage and control their employees. These processes will be concerned with a wide range of activities – the breadth of these activities will be examined in this chapter is concerned with understanding and experiencing a 'mainstreaming' approach to equal opportunities in public sector organisations. What these activities have in common is their intimate connection with people related aspects of management.

According to Dr. Needle:

> The production function is concerned with the creation of the goods and services offered to consumers. We refute that idea and examine the relationship of production with its environment by looking at the influences of a changing economy and government policy towards manufacturing industry, factors pertaining to the labour force, the impact of technological developments and cultural differences in the way societies view and organise production. [41]

Because organisation development is a generic term there are many possible ways in which it can be defined. The very broad meaning of organisation means that, for example, it can be related to French and Bell's idea on the behaviour science sense.

Organisation development is a long-term effort, led and supported by top management, to improve an organisation's visioning, empowerment, learning, and problem-solving processes, through an ongoing, collaborative management of organisation culture – with special emphasis on the culture of intact work teams and other team configurations – utilizing the consultant –facilitator role and the theory and technology of applied behavioural science, including action research. [42]

It was also suggested that the term 'organisational behaviour' is, strictly, a misnomer. The same caveat also applies to the term 'organisation development'. When we talk about organisation development it is important to emphasise a pluralistic approach and remember that, in practice, we are referring to the organisation development culture, conflict and change.

According to L. Mullins:

Organisation development (OD) is concerned with the diagnosis of organisational health and performance, and the ability of the organisation to adapt to change. It involves the applications of organisational behaviour and recognition of the social processes of the organisation. The manager needs to understand the nature of organisational culture and climate, employee commitment, conflict and the successful implementation of organisational change. [43]

To go along with any of the three scholars, one has to say that the organisation development programmes are aimed not only at improving organisation effectiveness and efficiency, but also at employee attitudes and morale which influence the level of performance. However, the emphasis of organisation development is more on the development of the organisation than the actual processes of organisation and management. Group members participate in discussions on the implications of the information, the diagnosis of problems and the development of action plans to help overcome the problems identified.

The objectives are to:

1. Gain insights into some of the political and practical problems surrounding the management of equal opportunities. It is therefore concerned with issues that are crucial to the consumer, issues of quantity, quality, availability and price; and issues that are crucial to the management of an enterprise, issues of productivity and cost.

2. Develop some of the skills of negotiating and managing equal opportunity policy. An important output is therefore a high level of customer satisfaction, both with the product and the service. Three kinds of feedback are important to this process; the customer's willingness to make return visits to the store; the careful research of customer needs; and the shop policy of accepting returned goods, which may then be repackaged and resold. The pursuit of quality is reflected in store layout and staff selection and training, but most significantly in the choice of supplier.

For example, Mullins refers to organisation development, with this statement: No two organisations are the same:

> Each organisation has its own types of problems and most appropriate remedies. Organisation development is action-oriented and tailored to suit specific needs. It takes a number of forms with varying levels of intervention. Organisation development concerns itself with the examination of organisational health and the implementation of planned change. This may include training in interpersonal skills, sensitivity training, and methods and techniques relating to motivational processes, patterns of communication, styles of leadership and managerial behaviour. 44

The emergence of this discipline or professional specialise within such organisations is, in many ways, due to the recognition of the importance of human relations issues in the total managements task. Although most of us will understand in our own minds what is meant by organisational culture, it is a general concept which is difficult to define or explain precisely. The concept of culture has developed from anthropology. It must be acknowledged, at this stage, that the areas of his or her responsibility are those where other managers, more directly concerned with production issues, also have a significant responsibility. Although people may not be aware consciously of culture, it still has a pervasive influence over their behaviour and actions.

According to T. Dawson, words:

> Performance appraisal – the increasing recognition afforded to the role of assessment of individual progress in both the motivation and reward processes. Again it must not be claimed that these issues are or should be the sole responsibility of the manager specifically charged with developing proper systems to manage these activities. For instances the operational manager is best placed to determine the skills required of new employees and hence needs to be intimately involved in the recruitment and selection and training processes. [45]

This study is concerned with our ability to develop, implement and review systems which maintain an environment where the best possible outcomes are achieved for all individuals in receipt of care. Culture is reinforced through the system of rites and rituals, patterns of communication, the informal organisation, expected patterns of behaviour and perceptions of the psychological contract. There is a particular need for market information and accurate predictions of demand. The most visible level of the culture is the constructed physical and social environment. This includes physical space and layout, the technological output, written and spoken language and the overt behaviour of group members.

This is obviously much easier where goods are made to order, less so when goods are made to stock. Solutions about how to deal with a new task, issue or problem are based on convictions of reality. If the solution works the value can transform into a belief. In this case historical data are important, but even this may prove inadequate in a highly volatile market of changing demand and high levels of competition. I remain when I have recently been appointed Practice Manager of an independent Care centre. My responsibilities include management and supervision of the local staff team comprising of 2 part time qualified care worker while the 12 staffs was unqualified. We are concerned here with two types of decision; the physical layout of the production system, and the design of individual jobs. Many of the issues pertinent to equipment design obtain here also and relate to the arrangement of equipment, work stations and people.

This was potentially difficult as a new manager had previously managed team and there was not an ethos of local management control. With this in mind I decided that the best approach was to immediately hold a meeting to acknowledge my role, the staffing approach I would wish to adopt and engage the team in identifying areas to be developed. The location of the production system in manufacturing industry is usually based upon a variety of factors including the proximity to raw materials and power supply, to transport systems for supply and distribution, to a labour market possessing the required skills.

Again, Dawson wrote this statement:

A brief observation of the ways in which organisations execute their human resource management challenges might suggest that, if the discipline has only just been recognised as one of importance in an enterprise, then there will be a tendency to afford this discipline through central departments – thus in infancy the discipline needs to be nurtured. However as the discipline receives wider acceptance in the organisation more decentralised deliveries might be acceptable and, at the extreme, there may be no need to employ any specific human resource professionals. [46]

It was through this process that I ensured each team member had a role in examine performance deficits, setting priorities and developing a service improvement programme. Through assessment and observation of working practices it was evident to me that there was a wide range of experience and skills across team members. Role or job description is often more important than the individual and position power is the main source of power. Task culture seeks to bring together the right resources and people, and utilises the unifying power of the group. Influence is widely spread and based more on expert power than on position or personal power. When a group of people decide that it is in their own interests to band together to do their own thing and share office space, equipment or clerical assistance then the resulting organisation would have a culture. In order to build on this and address both client staff individual and team performance improvements I have introduced and organised a programme of regular individual supervision and team development sessions. This provides the flexibility to focus on individual professional development and ensure the team works as an efficient, dynamic, complementary workforce.

In order to generate enthusiasm and motivation, I selected and allocated a number of task centred projects to team members. Different people enjoy working in different types of organisation culture and they are more likely to be happy and satisfied at work if their attributes and personalities are consistent with the culture of that part of the organisation in which they are employed. This provided the opportunity to undertake new areas of work, develop a new skill and contribute towards wider service development. It would also engender a sense of pride, ownership and expertise within some of the team. With National Registration requirements in mind, I have introduced a number of local standards for the centre.

It embraces a governing philosophy that all clients have the right to:
1. Privacy
2. Self-esteem
3. Fulfilment
4. Security of personal property
5. Dignity
6. Choice and control
7. Respect
8. Safety

It is important with my capacity to ensure the service remains client focused and that workers contributing to the care of individuals are aware of and enabled to integrate this philosophy in all aspects of daily living. In order to ensure services are designed and reviewed to promote and maximise the achievement of the best possible outcomes for individual client we and our workers need to be able to identify the best possible outcomes for an individual client, be aware of the factors which can mitigate against these outcomes being met and able to take appropriate action to facilitate the achievement of these outcomes. I have reviews and established monitoring systems to ensure reviews and reports are completed within timescales, correspondence is of a high professional standard and I have streamlined and upgraded the administration systems and introduced templates to ensure consistent quality and to support my staffs.

Ensuring them that:
    a. The services are designed, delivered and monitored in a way which promotes the achievement of the best possible outcomes for each of the individual clients.
    b. We provide opportunities for relevant people to inform us when the achievement of the best possible outcomes for an individual client is being adversely affected.
    c. Organisational factors, tensions and constraints, which impact upon the capacity of the service to promote the best possible outcomes for individuals are identified.
    d. Actions to improve the organisation's capacity to achieve the best possible outcomes for each of the individual clients are taken in line with the manager's level of authority and best practice.

Monitoring arrangements have not been limited to the immediate team and I have been involved in the development and implementation of an Agency wide Appraisal system. I now use formal assessment, structured supervision and personal development plans as part of my monitoring and assessing responsibilities. I have involved the staff team in the development of this performance appraisal system in order to ensure their commitment and ownership.

Legislation, policy and good practice:
1. National service standards and organisational policies and guidance which help to define the best possible outcomes for individuals.
2. The importance of ensuring clarity regarding the manager's role, level of accountability and authority and that of others in the individual's network.
3. Which client specific legislation informs and guides the identification and definition of the best possible outcomes for individual clients.
4. The types of organisational factors which might affect the achievement of the best possible outcomes for individual clients (such as staffing levels, shift patterns, policies and procedures etc.) and the acceptability or unacceptability of the constraints these places on achieving the best possible outcomes.
5. Methods to enhance communication between workers and clients, especially where there are differences in communication (e.g. English as a second language, sensory impairment, learning disability).
6. How to gather and record sufficient information to remain confident that the service is able to meet national service standards and best practice regarding the achievement of the best possible outcomes for individual clients.

I feel my style of managing performance at both an individual and team level, appropriately uses challenging targets to lift performance levels. I also place great emphasis upon individual personal development, which has contributed to improved competences and attitudes within the team and the achievement of goals and objectives. My management intervention has led to increased effective decision making, which has raised standards and confidence. This reflects, I feel, the combination of the supporting and directing leadership I apply to my managerial role.

Here are a few examples to give some ideas about the sort of evidence we might be able to find in our daily work.

    a.   Work activities: Meetings with relevant people to agree the best possible outcomes for individual clients. And care planning meetings, care conferences, reviews.

    b.   Products or outcomes: Correspondence, memos, files notes and minutes of above meetings. And working documents identifying client's needs and ways of meeting them.

Definition of Culture

Culture in an organization can be defined as a system of shared assumptions, values, beliefs and norms that governs the behaviour of individuals within the workplace. Within the organization however, there are four types of cultures that are dependent upon the needs of the environment and the strategic focus. This includes clan culture, bureaucratic culture, adaptability culture, as well as the mission culture. These can be broken down further depending on flexibility or stability, as well as how internal versus how external the work environment is. The English Dictionary defines the word culture has:

> The total of the inherited ideas, beliefs, values, and knowledge, which constitute the shared bases of social action.... [47]

Although most of us will understand in our own minds what is meant by "organisational culture", it is a general concept which is difficult to define or explain precisely. Although people may not be aware consciously of culture, it still has a pervasive influence over their behaviour and actions. Therefore, in one sense the position of manager is a formal recognition of success and as such managers play a key role in personifying the culture. Making many attitudes and ideas become permanent and unchallengeable, making them highly resistant to change.

W. L. French and C. H. Bell have pointed out that:

> Organisation development is a long-term effort, led and supported by top management, to improve an organisation's visioning, empowerment, learning, and problem-solving processes, through an ongoing, collaborative management of organisation culture – with special emphasis on the culture of intact work teams and other team configurations– utilizing the consultant-facilitator role and the theory and technology of applied behavioural science, including action research. [48]

Culture is reinforced through the system of rites and rituals patterns of communication, the informal organisation expected patterns of behaviour and perceptions of the psychological contract. This can be defined as an informal, unofficial, and in some cases, behind the scenes efforts made to influence an organization, increase power, or achieve other targeted objectives. Culture learning reflects someone's original values. Solutions about how to deal with a new task, issue or problem are based on convictions of reality. If the solution works the value can transform into a belief. Every organisation will have its own unique culture and most large businesses are likely to be something of a mix of cultures with examples for each of the four types in varying areas of the organisation.

Clan Culture

Clan culture is shaped between the dimensions of the organization's focus and dynamism, and as such, it possesses a high affiliation for teamwork and participation within the workplace. Cameron and Quinn made this statement:

> Therefore, assumed that this type of culture helped with employee development which has a long-term benefit not just for the company but also for the individuals themselves, and as such, an organization with such a culture can be held together through loyalty and tradition. This type of culture is more suited with a simple and stable environment, however as the company grows it is important to note that it can become more complex than before, changing the environment a low uncertainty to a low-moderate uncertainty. [49]

Bureaucratic Culture

The Bureaucratic culture is another type of culture in an organization, whereas the term bureaucracy itself is defined by scholars as the way in which people are organized by way of functional specialization, formal rules, laws, regulations and hierarchical relationships.

Alam made this statement:

> Therefore, saw the bureaucratic culture as a unique feature of government organizations consisting of generic features such as the management style being relatively authoritative, having a high degree of control, a top-down communication which can be seen as it being hierarchical with a centralized way of decision making, as well as limited initiatives and individuals searching for stability. In such a culture, leaders tend to be more control-oriented, which can be natively related to empowering leadership in the long-term. A Bureaucratic culture would be displayed in a stable and complex uncertainty depending on the type of organization due to the fact that the bureaucratic system is focused more on a Marxist perspective and as such tries to keep stability in the economy. [50]

Adaptability Culture

The Adaptability culture can be defined as a culture characterized by a strategic focus on the external environment through ways of flexibility and change in order to meet the demands of customers. According to Moorhouse the adaptability as the ability to learn new skills to respond effectively to evolving circumstances in the workplace:

> Adaptability culture was therefore viewed as crucial to future success in the workplace and as such, this type of culture is more suitable for organizations in a simple or a complex, but unstable environment. This means that this type of culture is highly aligned to a high-moderate uncertainty or a high uncertainty environment. [51]

The structure has also gotten more informal in some cases due to communication being based on collaborative teamwork. The ministry therefore now focusses on an innovative strategy rather than an efficiency strategy, in order to innovate ways in which the ministry itself and the people will survive through the pandemic while still being able to access an education system. There have also been fewer rules to cope with the system, however with the current changes both environmentally and technologically, the ministry has applied an adaptive culture.

Mission Culture

Lastly, the mission culture can be defined as a culture with a system of decentralized making, which is guided by a leader's intent and the guidelines within which individuals or teams of the workplace make well-informed and safety-conscious decisions in the most effective and efficient way possible. This type of culture within the organization is focused on continuous improvement and individual initiative. As it is believed, there should be a willingness to refine the framework based on evolving needs, as well as developing trust systems to emphasize on maximum situational awareness and analysis through the commitment of all actions benefiting to the desired team result. This type of culture has a high level of stability and is rather internal, resulting in a low uncertainty in the environment.

Craig Swenson wrote:

> Followers have historically been thought of as dependent individuals who need to be told what to do. Followership was therefore viewed as a passive role like clay awaiting the leader's creative force. 52

Flexible followers can adapt to changing demands and environments without being paralyzed by the stressful ambiguity that accompanies rapid change. In evaluating all four types of cultures, the stock exchange would consist of an adaptability culture as it would be mainly focused on trading stocks on the market which would be rather external as it organizes in such a way to drive organizational performance and success while ensuring high flexibility in a rather unstable environment. Leaders usually appreciate a sense of humour and they rate this quality highly in mission culture. While with charismatic leadership, however, the readiness my reflect follower's feelings of helplessness due to a perception that the situation is more than they can handle on their own.

The Types of Organisational Culture
This study describes the standards you should meet in carrying out your responsibility for developing, maintaining and evaluating systems to promote the rights, responsibilities

and diversity of people. The culture and structure of an organisation develop over time and in response to a complex set of factors. We can, however, identify a number of key influences that are likely to play an important role in the development of any corporate culture. In particular this should involve us in ensuring the promotion of participation and independence in order to facilitate the achievement of the best possible outcomes.

According to A. Kransdorff wrote:

> The reason, and manner in which, the organisation was originally formed, its age, and the philosophy and values of its owners and first senior managers will affect culture. A key event in the organisation's history such as a merger or major reorganisation, or a new generation of top management, may bring about a change in culture. Corporate history can be an effective induction tool to assist a growth programme, and to help integrate acquisitions and new employees by infusion with the organisation's culture and identity. [53]

It could be argued that the obtaining of the right type of employee is the most fundamental, requirement of good organisational management. The nature of the organisation's 'business' and its primary function have an important influence on its culture. This includes the range and quality of products and services provide the importance of reputation and the type of customers. Without the right type of employee any organisation cannot even begin to operate. However, the obtaining of the right calibre of employee is so often poorly or inadequately conducted. This is not such a simple question as it first appears. The primary function of the organisation will determine the nature of the technological processes and methods of undertaking work, which in turn also affect structure and culture. Rather the answering of this question evokes several answers and only after the management of an organisation has answered this question is it in a position to effectively recruit and select.

David Needle wrote this statement:

> The aim of scheduling is to balance the costs of production against demands for goods and services; to ensure that demand is met in the most efficient way possible. An important strategic consideration here is load-levelling, to ensure that the work is distributed as evenly as possible throughout the workforce, over the entire year, and making the most efficient use of available equipment. A whole series of theories and techniques have been developed to deal with such problems associated with the planning, scheduling and coordination of activities. These include queuing theory, linear programming and the more complex models of operational research. [54]

Although a business organisation may pursue profitability, this is not by itself very clear or a sufficient criterion for its effective management. To obtain the right people – this is the most obvious answer to the question. The geographical location and the physical characteristics can have a major influence on culture for examples, whether an organisation is located in a quiet rural location or a busy city centre. This can influence the types of customers and the staff employed. As has already been acknowledged an organisation which attracts the wrong type of person will not achieve its objectives as effectively as it might. It can also affect the nature of services provided, the sense of 'boundary' and distinctive identity, and opportunities for development. Thus, for instance, an organisation wishing to employ mechanical engineers would be well advised to seek and employ those people with the required mechanical engineering skills.

One needs to make sure that:

a. Those responsible for implementation are given appropriate levels of support to enable them to use the systems and structures effectively. All large organisations and most small organisations need to give considerable attention to the task of ensuring that their employees have the skills necessary to do their present job properly and to be able to fulfil other tasks in the organisation – which they may be required to do at short notice – well.

It is recorded by Peter Leyland and Terry Woods:

> Unfortunately, there is no universally accepted method of dividing it up, of objectively segregating one area of concern from another. Nevertheless, for convenience sake, we can list those activities that it conventionally concerns, e.g., social security, health, housing, planning, education, immigration, the exercise

of powers by central and local government and the police, tribunals and inquiries. You will also notice that these roughly correspond to the main activities of the modern state. In so far as it is possible to identify a common body of rules and procedures that apply in these areas, such rules, taken together, form the basis of what we call administrative law. [55]

b. Breaches of confidentially are investigated and the appropriate action is taken to limit any damage. Firstly organisations are train so that those doing the jobs can do them successfully. Obviously there is no point in giving someone a job to do if that person does not have the appropriate skills to do that job. If the person is not trained any money injected into the production process will be money wasted.

c. Where information is to be provided to those in another agency, it is confirmed that the recipient has the necessary systems and resources to maintain the confidentially of the information. Doing a job better – sometimes people are capable of doing the job but they would do the job better if they received some training. In addition this point acknowledges the circumstances where long standing employees might need to adjust to changes in production technology – that is few, if any jobs have fixed skill content.

d. Factors which indicate risk to an individual's physical or psychological health are understood and can be correctly identified, by all those for whom the manager is responsible. Sometimes the need to provide a safe work environment may constitute a major consideration in the decision to train an employee. Some jobs are dangerous and to ensure that the job is done well and that all hazards are avoided some training may be needed. This factor can be seen to be particularly important when public service employees provide a service where, unless the job is done carefully, the public itself may be in danger – e.g. driving a train.

e. By ensuring everyone within the agency is empowered to report abusive behaviour, suspicions of abuse or potential risk of harm to self or others. When an organisation has established what its manpower needs are, it is then in an position to assess its current manpower resources. Only if its current resources fail to match those required in its manpower plan should an organisation decide to recruit. In many ways under such circumstances training would be the most desired option since it may be a more effective way of enhancing levels of motivation within the organisation.

There are, however, many other ways in which people attempt to describe and understand what constitutes organisational culture, and different areas of attention for analysing the elements of culture. For example, certain groups and individuals are particularly vulnerable to abuse of specific kinds, such as neglect or fraud. Abuse may be neglect, civil rights violations, failure to protect property, physical, emotional, psychological, financial, sexual or through the denial of rights or choice. It may also be abuse of the individual or their property. Harm may be caused to the individual by others in their network (including families, friends, other residents or workers), by the physical environment where the service is provided or by organisations due to institutionalised discrimination.

Tony Dawson made this statement:

> Employing anyone who applies – it must be acknowledged that in certain occupations at certain times the selection method need not be too sophisticated. For instance in certain manual jobs in times of full employment the mere physical size and strength of an individual gives sufficient evidence to justify employment. It must be recognised that, although this strategy is possible, it should be adopted only after due thought has been given to the possible consequences. [56]

Hence it is necessary to design a form which allows the interviewer to record the appropriate responses of the candidates. Naturally this recording should be done in such a way as to guarantee accuracy whilst not distracting the candidate. In addition it may well be that different people are skilled in enquiring into different aspects of the candidate's suitability for the job. Within reason the more people involved the less danger there will be of undue bias or unfairness entering into the process. The factors:

1. Signs and symptoms of harm, abuse or failure to protect. Excellent leaders are not merely aware of the organisation's basic assumptions, they also know how to take action and mould and refine them.

2. The different types and patterns of social and emotional behaviours which might result in abuse, harm or failure to protect. What is much more common today is the widespread recognition that organisational change is not just, or even necessarily mainly, about changing the structure but often requires changing the culture too.
3. The types and impact of organizational factors on the likelihood of harm, abuse and failure to protect (such as staffing levels, recording policies), acceptable and unacceptable organizational constraints.
4. Factors which inhibit clear communication about indicators or suspicion of abuse (e.g. fear of whistle blowing, peer group pressure etc) and how to minimise them.

According Dr. Leyland and Dr. Woods:

> In providing answers to these questions, we start by recognising that any system of law operates in a pluralistic society, one comprised of a multitude of public bodies and institutions. It is made up of individuals who have interests associated with their profession or occupation, their class or ethnicity; individuals who hold varied political and social opinions. If we accept this, it follows that there can be no single, coherent perspective which underpins public law, in either theory or practice. As we proceed, it will become increasingly evident to the attentive reader that these varied perspectives colour both the formulation of the law and the decisions that emanate from it. [57]

We argued then that the relationship also involved a number of other variables such as strategy, culture and the behaviour of interest groups. In addition to arrangements for the carrying out of organisational processes, management has a responsibility for creating a climate in which people are motivated to work willingly and effectively. Some of these forces are better understood than others.

Culture as a Learnt Entity
We live in a culture which is crying out for effective leaders. "What are the cultures?" is a question being asked in business, government, education – and even in the church. Culture managers come may name. Titles include Chief Culture Officer, Chief People Officer; Vice President of Culture; Vice President of Diversity, Equity and Inclusion; and Head of Employee Experience to name a few. This is a relatively new role as companies realize that investing in culture returns significant financial impact (ROI). Often in smaller organizations this isn't a full-time role, but rather a responsibility of the Human Resource (HR) team.

I would suggest that this study is not an ordinary cultural theory. I believe that our world desperately needs Christian leaders, managers, management etc., who lead like Jesus Christ. Depending on the circumstances, differing members of the team may take starring or leaderships roles. This elevation of team, personal bonding, and leadership, or managerial or management by gift hardly represents a new theme in literature or art. Nevertheless, the emphasis on individual giftedness or talent driving the leadership, managerial or management of a particular situation reflects a shift in general leadership, managerial or management philosophy.

George Weber emphasizes that "the historic command structure organization is dead" and reminds us that:

> The successful leader of the future must have one more attribute that weights perhaps as much as all the others on the scale of effectiveness; he or she must be a tireless, inventive, observant, risk taking, and ever hopeful builder and enabler of management and leadership teams within and among the organization's constituent parts. [58]

Is this biblical? Many churches and Christian organizations have practiced authoritative, visionary leadership, managers and management, top-down administrative policies since their inception, and have prospered in the doing. Does culture have a place in the church? Jesus Christ introduced radically different kind of leadership roles, managerial, pastoral and management skills when He begin to teach His disciples about culture in His Kingdom. Regardless of the title or role, the activity of culture management sits at the intersection of the entire organization. A great corporate culture influences (and is influenced by) the organization's leadership, organization's goals and strategy, HR, IT... even the design of the office or remote setup. This different kind role has a huge impact on the bottom line of the business.

Management culture is a collection of leadership norms and practices that emerge from a firm's history and leadership. It is a sub-component of organizational culture that describes management realities beyond official policy and procedure. Management culture may include both political climate and expectations related to measurement, quality, innovation, spending, learning from failure and management style. Example, "the rulers of the Gentiles lord it over them, and their high officials exercise authority over them". As we know, "lording over" and "exercising authority" are still being practiced all around us – even in the church. Jesus taught clearly that approach was inappropriate for His kingdom. Without a doubt, our Lord is calling us to a distinctively Christ-centered kind of leadership, managerial, pastoral and management cultural theory. Part of it has to do with the way we use the authority of leadership, managerial and management. Listen to Lawrence Richards:

> Essentially, the authority of leaders today is a moral authority, a freedom of action extended to them by God, to influence the people of God to respond to Christ's moral authority. ... It is right and proper for secular governments to demand, and compel, obedience. [59]

Not in rebellion, but in a genuine effort to find a better or other way. On the other hand, a public relation respects truth and goes about its task with dignity and good manners, recognizing its responsibility to the various publics involved and engaging in cooperation at all points. We make needs known, we clarify objectives, and ministry or companies proceeds on the assumption that people respond intelligently and willingly when they feel a part of our organization philosophy. While many managers do not deny the importance of organizational culture in employee satisfaction, few fail to realize the direct impact they have in shaping it. It is oftentimes believed that cultures are predetermined; however, this is a false assumption. It is crucial that managers at all levels are aware of their roles and responsibilities in upholding positive workplace environments that can increase employee's satisfaction. Dissatisfaction is the major cause of poor turnover and can have detrimental cost and environmental effects on the agency.

To take advantage of methods like dialogue and to improve its way of thinking, the team must also change its language. The language the team uses greatly influences the quality of ideas generated and the willingness of team members to share those ideas; in some cases, technology works, whereas in others, it doesn't – as illustrated in the previous examples. In the rush to go global, corporations are requiring their managers to be effective across distances and cultures never before mastered. This theme looks at learning as a critical component in organizational culture. As such, the focus is on "the way we do things here" or "the way we think about things around here".

In general, these definitions focus on the way we act and the way we think. In this regard, a widely accepted definition of culture is that of Schein:

> The pattern of basic assumptions that a given group has invented, discovered, or developed in learning to cope with its problems of external adaption and internal integration, and that have worked well enough to be considered valid, and, therefore to be taught to new members as the correct way to perceive, think, and feel in relation to those problems. [60]

We will see more in detail Schein's view later on in this article. This model will give us a framework through which we can evaluate the various forms of information technology and how they apply to team interaction. What is essential is to understand the effects of this approach: Culture is taught to new members as a way of behaving that is "correct" for the specific organization. In this sense, Culture becomes a self-perpetuating feature for organizational survival and growth. Also, a consequence of this view is that the visible artefacts of Culture are distilled down to the behaviors that people teach to others as they join the organization. The implication of this theme is a strong focus on strategy development as a cultural activity. The basic assumption is that beliefs impact the definition of strategy. This is why the definition of a strategy needs to take into consideration the cultural aspects, and need to have a storytelling component. We do not attempt to provide a country of the art review on types of information technology; our purpose is to identify the considerations that managers must wrestle with when attempting to bring together groups of people who are not in the same place.

Culture as a Belief System

Another useful way to improve team thinking culture is through a process that challenges the current assumptions of the organization example for Miller's Bible College and Institution. A team conversation with this focus begins by clarifying the culture assumptions that the organization holds about the problem or issue presented. Take this assumption about what it takes to train or teach students at the Bible College. If the team challenges this assumption, they would say that you do not need a license to teach at Church Bible colleges in the city or the country into the church building.

The team could then discuss what would happen if the church licenses were eliminated and how the impact would be different for different types of licenses. The results might be that the team recommends that several licensing processes simply be abolished. It cannot be imposed, it cannot be initiated by others, and it can be withdrawn.

Managers are always under the magnifying glass, with each action carefully scrutinized by subordinates. They must exercise caution when making decisions, ensuring that fairness and equitability exists among staff, and that ethical standards are upheld on a continual basis. The four cultural components, viewed as managerial traits of trust and trustworthiness, empowerment, consistency and mentorship coexist at all times regardless of the type of culture. Managers must put support systems and other mechanisms into place that allow employees the opportunity to empower themselves and to flourish, thus increasing their own effectiveness as well as that of the organization.

G. White wrote:

> In the current industrial climate, there needs to be concern not only for producing goods or services, but also for the encouragement of innovate, exploratory and creative ideas that go beyond what can be prescribed for the job, and for the application to work of intuitive as well as explicit knowledge. These multiple objectives can only be achieved if managers consider with care exactly what kinds of commitment they are aiming for, and design policies and practices accordingly. [61]

However, Bible College organizations should develop new ways to increase the loyalty and commitment of employees. Different cultures breed different employee experiences. There's no standard set of organizational values to adopt. Yet the cultural elements and management processes should all signal the expected behavior inside each employee's interaction. This includes attention to reward strategies based on recognition of contribution rather than status or position, systematic training and development including the skills for working in cross-functional teams; and the training of teachers and staffs in counseling, coaching and leadership skills. Often cultivating organizational culture means implementing cultural change. Changing the wheels on a moving car is much harder than doing so before the car has momentum. The earlier that leadership creates shared assumptions and displays leadership behaviors that reinforce the assumptions, the more likely the company's culture will be pointed toward a healthy environment.

A new psychological contract needs to consider the Bible College of the future. This is the view expressed by many scholars. According to Altman, Cooper and Garder:

> The old command and control interpretation of loyalty in the workplace need to be replaced with an attitude of commitment by both sides which leads to a more pragmatic relationship within the limited horizons against which business are being managed today worldwide. [62]

The ability to create new organizational forms and processes, to innovate in both the technical and organizational arenas, is crucial to remaining competitive in an increasingly turbulent world. But this kind of organizational learning requires not only the invention of new forms but also their adoption and diffusion to the other relevant parts of the organization and to other organizations in a given industry. Organizations still have not learned how to manage that process. The examples of successful organizational learning we have seen either tend to be short-run adaptive learning — doing better at what we are already doing — or, if they are genuine innovations, tend to be isolated and eventually subverted and abandoned.

As the Bible College team challenges its current culture assumptions, it begins to look for new ways to do things that are outside those assumptions. Just because the team challenges an assumption does not mean that it cannot, in the end, validate that assumption. However, in the exploration all the themes have something in common: the idea that several deeply rooted assumptions influence the behaviors of the members of an organization. This is why Culture is often described using the iceberg metaphor, by which it is underlined that there is a large number of components that are not visible but influence the visible "tip of the iceberg". This metaphor was first proposed in 1976 by E.T. Hall, and despite some critiques, it still is an excellent illustration of a complex concept.

For example, Drucker makes the following point:

> Any business enterprise must build a true team and weld individual efforts into a common effort. Each member of the enterprise contributes something different, but they must

all contribute towards a common goal. Their efforts must all pull in the same direction, and their contributions must fit together to produce a whole – without gaps, without friction, without unnecessary duplication of effort… If these requirements are not met, managers are misdirected. Their efforts are wasted. Instead of teamwork, there is friction, frustration and conflict. 63

The act, in and of itself, was nothing extraordinary. It was what everyone did if they wanted to gather a group of people together for debate, discussion, fellowship and work. I am reminded of Martin Luther, who was comfortable with not even being sure of some of the statements on the 92 pages documents because discussing their validity was his motivation for posting them. They detail the gathering of scientific inquiry and data, new research and investigation, and actual construction of the conceptual theory. Strauss and Sayles give this summarizes:

The experimenters called the factors which lead to this rather sterile, non-involved attitude… We shall accordingly call management which emphasizes these factors… Such a "be good" policy may provide a pleasant environment in which to work and a considerable amount of around the job satisfaction, but little satisfaction through the job, and little sense of enthusiasm or creativity. 64

Once again, we can be helped by the work of secular research. Christian organisations need to emphasize the satisfiers of achievement, responsibility, and advancement. But surely our primary deficiency does not lie here, but in our failure to recognize the presence of dissatisfiers. Too often we concentrate our attention on multiplying and enhancing the satisfiers, while the dissatisfiers may be chipping away at the morale, and consequently the motivation, of our people. Surely Christian theology teaches us to recognize that the inner factors of a leader's attitude toward personnel, self, leadership and management team will represent a crucial role in service performance.

Zaleznik wrote:

> One of the few management theoreticians who seek to place responsibility upon the worker rather than constantly harping on changing the organization. His position emphasizes an internal view of humanity and attempts to show how people, by the strength of their character and personality, can remake organizations… others with whom they interact, the organization within which they and their groups work, and the cultures in which they all live. [65]

Culture as an Independent Variable

Culture helps to account for variations among organizations and managers, both nationally and internationally. It helps to explain why different groups of people perceive things in their own way and perform things differently from other groups. This constitutes organizational culture, and different areas of attention for analyzing the element of culture. These culture and structure of an organization develop over time and in response to a complex set of factors. With greater international competition, an understanding of national culture has become of increasing importance for managers. For example, Wilson has suggested:

> That culture is a characteristic of the organisation, not of individuals. One way to examine the culture of an organisation is to look at its corporate image to see what and who is valued in the organisation. The corporate image provides a mental picture that clients, customers, employees and others have of an organisation. [66]

Cultural practices vary widely among different countries and because of our own values may be, difficult to understand. When we begin teaching or working a new group or an individual, there will be lots of information you must explain regarding your organization, the facilities available and the programmer. Our organization might have a checklist of general points for us to follow and we may need to add specific points regarding our subject and the learning environment. The concept itself of Culture is a concept that triggers many discussions among different social scientists on precisely what it is, how it is defined, how it forms, how it evolves, and what it truly means for individuals. When we apply this concept to organizations, we trigger even bigger quarrels on its exact meaning, despite the many activities done in the name of culture change. As with the previous articles of this series, I will try to represent the existing complexity of the topic, once again showing that it is impossible to find a correct answer. The key lesson, as with the previous issues of leadership, is that we need to find consistency in what this topic means, in the framework of our international design effort. However, all members of staff help to shape the dominant culture of an organization, irrespective of what senior management feels it should be.

As mentioned, there are many different definitions of Organizational Culture; perhaps the most known one is "the way we do things around here" may be difficult to understand. When we begin teaching or working with a new way, many of the definitions have been focused on identifying and listing the key components and elements of organizations cultures. For example, if the organization operates within a dynamic environment, it requires a structure and culture that are sensitive and readily adaptable to change. An organic structure is more likely to respond effectively to new opportunities and challenges, and risks and limitations presented by the external environment. Many elements can be included on the definition: organization's expectations, experiences, philosophy, as well as the values that guide member behaviors and is expressed in member self-image, inner workings, interactions with the outside world, and future expectations. Culture is based on shared attitudes, beliefs, customs, and written and unwritten rules that have been developed over time and are considered valid but the organization's members.

Culture as a Dependent Variable
At the heart of Bible College organization development and improved performance is the need for effective management. It is the role of management to act as an integrating activity and to coordinate, guide and direct the efforts of members towards the achievement of goals and

objectives. As such Culture can be crafted into something "positive" for the organization, through specific change initiatives. The pervasive nature of organizational culture means that if change is to be brought about successfully this is likely to involve changes to culture. For example, Stewart makes the following comment on the relationship between culture and change.

> In recent years attention has shifted from the effects of the organisation of work on people's behaviour to how behaviour is influenced by the organisational culture. What is much more common today is the widespread recognition that organisational change is not just, or even necessarily mainly, about changing the structure but often requires changing the culture too. [67]

Culture can help reduce complexity and uncertainly. This line of thought makes intervention on Culture more complicated, but no less desirable. It provides a consistency in outlook and values, and makes possible processes of decision-making, coordination and control. Mainly because the resulting understanding is that firms that have cultures supportive of strategy are likely to be successful, while firms that have insufficient "fit" between strategy and Culture must change since it is the Culture which supports the strategy. For example, in commenting on Heineken's superiority in world markets, Heller makes the point that it rests in part on its remarkable corporate culture:

> There is nothing accidental about cultural
> strengths… There is a relationship between an
> organisation's culture and its performance [68]

In practical terms, this approach sees activities as how to mould and shape internal culture theory in particular ways and how to change culture, consistent with managerial purposes. All the organizations are very demanding of the people who work for them but this a balanced by a nurturing culture which show that they also care for their employees in numerous ways.

Chapter Four
The Nature of Organisational Behaviour

Introduction

We live in an organizational world. Organizations of one form or another are a necessary part of our society and serve many important needs. The decisions and actions of management in organizations have an increasing impact on individuals, other organizations and the community. Within these organisations, people are keys and underpin everything within it and ultimately, its success or failure. This happens through many different dynamics with two of them discussed in this report being the internal environment and leadership from management.

These are of the most important dynamics which affect also Miller's Bible College and Institution. These dynamics interlink well as creating a positive internal environment stem from how the management deals with its employees. It is important, therefore, to understand how organisations function and the pervasive influences which they exercise over the behaviour of people. If both manger and employees work together then it builds the foundation for a long lasting, successful and most importantly profitable organization whose employees are fully invested and dedicated to the organizational behaviour.

Organizational behaviour is concerned with the study of the behaviour of people within an organizational setting.

It involves the understanding, prediction and control of human behaviour. If these accepts are not dealt with then this can lead to inefficiencies in productivity hindering the performance of a firm. Internal environment and leadership are often forgotten about being covert in nature with mangers underestimating the impact these can have on performance in both the short and long run. When the climate is healthy then it should improve an organisation's effectiveness by clear interactions leading to everyone working to the same common goal. However, it is important that all employees are on board. One negative employee can have a chain reaction among a team. It is the job of a manger to see if this is happening and deal with the root cause as quickly as possible to stop the chain reaction from starting.

In Miller's Bible College and Institution, their internal environment is very strong and positive with them working hard for each other. A great example of team spirit was shown during staffs training when the college came together. A further aspect of creating a beneficial internal environment comes from the effect of external college encroaching into organisation. This will always happen as no organisation acts in isolation so is going to be affected in some way. A way organisation can minimise the impact of this is through environmental scanning. This is a systematic method of monitoring changes in an organisation's business environment.

Definition of Organizational Behaviour
This area of study examines human behaviour in a work environment and determines its impact on job structure, performance, communication, motivation, leadership, etc. To be the best leaders, mangers should lead by example

and have regard for the need to motivate the people under their charge. As a result, employees will have a greater willingness to be more productive and work harder for their manger which will consequently boost output and performance of the whole organization. Organizational behaviour is a combination of responses to external and internal stimuli by a person as an individual or as a part of a group. This is a brief introductory tutorial that explains the methodologies applied in the rapidly growing area of organizational behaviour in an organization. The term "organizational behaviour" can be defined as the scientific study and practical application of knowledge concerning the way in which individuals and groups of individuals act and behave within an organization, in which they work. The study also includes the interaction between members of the organization and the external environment. Mullins wrote:

> Organizations are made up of their individual members. The individual is a central feature of organizational behaviour and a necessary part of any behavioural situation, whether acting in isolation or as part of a group, in response to expectations of the organization, or as a result of the influences of the external environment. It is the task of management to provide a working environment which permits the satisfaction of individual needs as well as the attainment of organizational goals. [69]

The study becomes organizational behaviour is very interesting and challenging too. It is related to individual, group of people working together in teams. This study organisational behaviour more challenging when situational factors interact. The study of organizational behaviour relates to the expected behaviour of an individual in the organization. We have looked at a variety of organizational behaviour issues which can be applied to a range of organizational settings and in doing so we have highlighted the importance of the individual in the workplace. The personality of an individual is important and understanding here allows for behaviour to one end of the spectrum, a manger can be autocratic where the focus is total power with the manger. The key is that the manger purposely gives up control so that freedom of action occurs and he can get on with his own job. The manger will always listen to his employees in order to make the correct decision for the team. Leadership traits include charismatic, inspiring and high energy.

For leadership to be affective and boost the performance of organisation there needs to be both the willingness of the manger to help and support his team and also for his team to ask for the help. It works both ways. This will in turn be motivational for the whole team and removes any obstacles that could hinder meeting goals such as misconceptions or miscommunications. No two individuals are likely to behave in the same manner in a particular work situation. Managers, leadership or management under whom an individual is working should be able to explain, predict, evaluate and modify human behaviour that will largely depend upon knowledge, skill and experiences of the manager, leader or management in handling large group of people in diverse situations.

Organizational behaviour is the study of human behaviour in organizational settings, the interface between human behaviour and the organization, and the organization itself. Organizational behaviour is a normative science also. While positive science discusses the only cause-effect relationship, organizational behaviour prescribes how the findings of applied research can be applied to socially accept organizational goals. Organizational behaviour is the application of knowledge about how people, individuals, and groups act and react in an organization, in order to reach and accomplish the highest quality of performances, and dominant results.

Thus, organizational behaviour deals with what is accepted by individuals and society engaged in an organization. Yes, it is not that organizational behaviour is not normative at all. In fact, organization behaviour is normative as well which is well underscored by the proliferation of management theories. We have reviewed major individual differences that effect employee attitude and organization. The study of organizational behaviour is one of the most significant elements in the management sciences, as it makes management learn from what has succeeded elsewhere. Generally, financial strength is a measure of the organizations past success. Ronald R. Sims wrote:

> What determines whether the organization will continue to deliver sought-after products, will continue to develop cutting edge technology, will continue to make the right options about which direction the market is going to go, will continue to make sound investments, is the people and the organizational culture and structure. Different organizational structures will show different types of organizations that

each has strengths and weaknesses. Human beings encourage seeking satisfaction in every phase of their life. From satisfying their basic primal needs and wants, which is hunger, thirst, rest and social interaction, the complex community today has its benchmark of goals and fulfilment that should be accomplished by individuals. [70]

The industrial revolution led to significant social and cultural change, including new forms of organization. Organizational behaviour can be defined as the understanding, prediction and management of human behavior both individually or in a group that occur within an organization. Internal and external perspectives are the two theories of how organizational behaviour can be viewed from an organization's point of view. In this tutorial, we will be learning in detail about both the theories. It is the systematic study and application of knowledge about how individuals and groups act within the organizations where they work. Organizational behaviour draws from other disciplines to create a unique field. For example, when we review topics such as personality and motivation, we will again review studies from the field of psychology. The topic of team processes relies heavily on the field of sociology.

Importance of Organization Behaviour People's Side
While working in an organization, it is very important to understand others behaviour as well as make others understand ours. In order to maintain a healthy working environment, we need to adapt to the environment and understand the goals we need to achieve. This can be done easily if we understand the importance of organizational

behaviour. The study of organizational behaviour ultimately looks at the people side of the organization and does so in order to address how we can manage employees by looking at, and understanding why people act as they do in organizations. By looking at the interaction amongst the formal dynamics of the organization and the people within it, organizational behaviour is concerned with the micro foundations: the importance of people, how they think, how they behave and the interactions they have with each other.

Organizational behaviour draws on both managers and employee perspectives and does so to draw out the nature of the organization as an inherently complex, messy and emotional place as Miller's Bible College and Institution believes. This was the same view of Ronald Sims.

Ronald R. Sims again wrote:

> This selective set of fulfilment and goals encloses securing a good job, preferably with a good pay and hopefully, with a high level of job satisfaction. There is no fixed and formal guideline on how to overcome challenges at work into a motivation for individuals to reach job satisfaction, so that with the good practicing of organizational behaviour development, individuals are able to well handle the task pressure, and overcome the variety of challenges. Organizational behaviour is the application of knowledge about how peoples, individuals, and groups act and react in an organization, in order to reach and accomplish the highest quality

of performances, and dominant results. One way for an organization to become more innovative is to capitalize on its own employees to innovate. All organizations and groups experience the direct relationship between job satisfaction, and performance. [71]

The homothetic approach has value, as it is applicable to organizations due to its efficient way of capturing the personality profiles of individual employees. By quantifiably measuring personality it is possible to ascertain if an individual has a low, average or high level of a given trait which can be useful when matching employees within a working team. This efficient manner of viewing personality has made personality and the study of such translatable into the workplace which has built an important bridge between theory and practice. Ideographic conceptualizations of personality approach personality from a more tacit open to interpretation examination of an individual's personality. The idiographic approach views personality as something which cannot be measured in a quantitative manner and instead, the personality of an individual needs to be examined in a social setting thus opening up the nature versus nurture debate. Using research methods such as interviews and observations, the idiographic perspective offers a broader approach to personality which views personality as being a fluid entity which cannot be fixed or tied down.

According to Costa & McCrae:

The study of personality is a complex topic and one, which comprises different perspectives thus requiring evaluation from different angles. Within the study of personality, two perspectives exist the homothetic approach and the idiographic approach. The homothetic approach is the dominant way of viewing personality which views personality as a quantifiable science by looking at examining traits. Traits can be defined as 'a set of behavioural, emotional and cognitive tendencies that people display over time and across situations and that distinguish individuals from one another. [72]

The team realized that higher management did not understand the value of early problem identification and continued to use its new learning, assuming that the ultimate results would speak for themselves. The team was able to complete the design well ahead of schedule and with considerably lower costs, but, contrary to expectations, higher managers never understood the reasons for these notable results nor gave the team credit for having learned a new way of solving problems. Instead, higher managers gave themselves credit for having gotten the team "under control." They did not consider the team to be particularly innovative and disbanded it. The personality of an individual is important and understanding here allows for behaviour to be examined and hopefully predicted within the firm. At this individual level, we need to be able to measure personality and therefore psychometric tests have a variety of tools which can be used. Such tools must however be approached with caution to ensure they are not used to solely base decisions on an individual's capability. This is due to what we know about an individual being so much more than their personality alone.

The two scholars Costa & McCrae have said that:

> The two approaches which exist to personality:
> the homothetic and the idiographic both view
> personality in a different way and this can be
> argued to result in a particular trade-off. For
> example, the more time that is available the
> richer the picture we are able to gain of an
> individual whom may for example allow for
> the individuals personality to be ascertained
> through detailed appraisals and interviews.
> When less time is available, more efficient
> tools have to be used and thus whilst they
> may result in a more abstract appraisal of an
> individual, they are a valuable tool within
> large organizations. [73]

Following points bring out the importance of organization
behaviour –

- It helps in explaining the interpersonal relationships
  employees share with each other as well as with their
  higher and lower subordinates.
- It balances the cordial relationship in an enterprise by
  maintaining effective communication.
- It assists in marketing.
- It helps in making the organization more effective.

Thus, studying organizational behaviour helps in
recognizing the patterns of human behaviour and in turn
throws light on how these patterns profoundly influence the
performance of an organization. An organization consists
of people with different traits, personality, skills, qualities,

interests, background, beliefs, values and intelligence. In order to maintain a healthy environment, all the employees should be treated equally and be judged according to their work and other aspects that affect the firm. All organizations function within a given internal and external environment. Internal environment can be defined as the conditions, factors, and elements within an enterprise that influences the activities, choices made by the organization, and especially the behaviour of the employees. While external environment can be defined as outside factors that affect the organization's ability to operate. Some of them can be manipulated by the organization's marketing, while others require the organization to make adjustments.

<u>Nature of People</u>
In simple words, nature of people is the basic qualities of a person, or the character that personifies an individual they can be similar or unique. Talking at the organizational level, some major factors affecting the nature of people have been highlighted.

Laurie J. Mullins

> The behaviour of people, however, cannot be studied in isolation. It is necessary to understand interrelationships with other variables which together comprise the total organization. To do this involves consideration of interactions among the formal structure, the tasks to be undertaken, the technology employed and methods of carrying out work, the process of management and the external environment. [74]

Individual Difference – It is the managerial approach towards each employee individually, that is one-on-one approach and not the statistical approach, that is, avoidance of single rule. Example– Manager should not be biased towards any particular employee rather should treat them equally and try not to judge anyone on any other factor apart from their work. A whole person – as we all know that a person's skill or brain cannot be employed in isolation, therefore, we have to employee a whole person. Skill comes from background and knowledge. Our personal life cannot be totally separated from our work life, just like emotional conditions are not separable from physical conditions. So, people function is the functioning of a total human being not a specific feature of human being.

The Culture and Organisation Behaviour

In this chapter we have reviewed major individual differences that affect employee attitudes and behaviour. Our values and personality explain our preferences and the situations we feel comfortable with. Personality may influence our behavior, but the importance of the context in which behaviour occurs should not be neglected. Many organizations use personality tests in employee selection, but the use of such tests is controversial because of problems such as faking and low predictive value of personality for job performance. Perception is how we interpret our environment. It is a major influence over our behaviour, but many systematic biases color our perception and lead to misunderstandings. For example, many organizations espouse "team-work" and "cooperation," but the behaviour that the incentive and control systems of the organization reward and encourage is based more on a shared tacit assumption that only individuals can be accountable and that the best results come from a system of individual competition and rewards.

If the external situation demands teamwork, the group will develop some behaviour that looks, on the surface, like teamwork by conducting meetings and seeking consensus, but members will continue to share the belief that they can get ahead by individual effort and will act accordingly when rewards are given out. I have heard many executives tell their subordinates that they expect them to act as team but remind them in the same sentence that they are all competing for the boss's job! Nature of organization states the motive of the organization. It is the opportunities it provides in the global market. It also defines the employees' standard; in short, it defines the character of the organization by acting as a mirror reflection of the organization. We can understand the nature of any firm with its social system, the mutual interest it shares and the work ethics.

Let us take a quick look at all these factors −
Social system: Every organization socializes with other organizations, their customers, or simply the outer world, and all of its employees - their own social roles and status. Their behaviour is mainly influenced by their group as well as individual drives. Social systems are of two types namely.

Mutual interest: Every organization needs people and people need organizations to survive and prosper. Basically, it's a mutual understanding between the organization and the employees that help both reach their respective objectives. Example − we deposit our money in the banks in return the bank gives us loan, interest, etc.

<u>Ethics:</u> They are the moral principles of an individual, group, and organization. In order to attract and keep valuable employees, ethical treatment is necessary and some moral standards need to be set. In fact, organizations are now establishing code of ethics training reward for notable ethical behaviour.

The Managerial Behaviour in Organisation
Human nature is the common quality of all human being; people naturally behave according to certain principles of human nature. Human needs are an important part of human nature. Values, beliefs, and custom, differ from country to country and even within group to group, but in general, all people have a few basic needs. As a manager or leader, we must understand these needs because they can be powerful motivations. In the same way, middle management and higher levels will develop their own shared assumptions and, at each level, will teach those assumptions to newcomers as they get promoted. These hierarchically based cultures create the communication problems associated with "selling senior management on a new way of doing things," or "getting budget approval for a new piece of equipment," or "getting a personnel requisition through."

As each cultural boundary is crossed, the proposal has to be put into the appropriate language for the next higher level and has to reflect the values and assumptions of that level. Or, from the viewpoint of the higher levels, decisions have to be put into a form that lower levels can understand, often resulting in "translations" that actually distort and sometimes even subvert what the higher levels wanted. Applying and controlling through these factors will give a positive grip on managerial behaviours in workplace.

For example if a manager "can organise teamwork and motivate people for working with him on difficult new task under time pressure". There are underlying assumption concerning his or her knowledge and attitudes needed for work planning communicating with people and motivating, and organising team, while respecting strict time schedules. Basically speaking, the skills involved in managerial jobs include technical subject skills, general management an organisation skill, analytical subject skills, social and cultural skills, management of people, communication and leadership skills, and political skills.

The managerial effectiveness at first, I have to define as the goal and achieving behaviour. Managerial effectiveness is achieved, if a person is an effective manager. An effective manager is one who is positive in his personality, his managerial process and the results of his process. One of the main attributes that will contribute to the managerial effectiveness is leadership. And this is also defined in terms of the quantity and quality of standards of performance and the satisfaction and commitment of subordinates. The managerial effectiveness also follows the organizational main goal, which is concerned with doing the right thing and relates to outputs of the business and what the manager actually achieves. Management effectiveness must relate to the achievement of some purpose, objective or task to the performances of the process of management and the execution of work.

Chapter Five

Understanding the Roles in Organisational Skills

Organisational Skills Definition

In today's highly competitive job market, employers and hiring managers are often looking for more than just the basic skills needed to do a job. Skills like communication, planning, etc and detail orientation are vital for keeping pace with rapidly evolving industries. Making organisational skills are those related to creating structure and order, boosting productivity, and prioritizing tasks that must be completed immediately, versus those that can be postponed, delegated to another person, or eliminated altogether.

Peter Senge defined it as a place:

> Where people continually expand their capacity to create the results, they truly desire, where new and expansive patterns of thinking are nurtured, where collective aspiration is set free, and where people are continually learning how to learn together. [75]

The learning organisation sounds ideal; the kind of company in which we might all like to work! The picture that is painted of this type of organisation skills is one that is ultimately highly flexible and open-ended. It is able to continually transform itself and learn from experience and thus always be ready to take advantage of changing external conditions. Such an organisation like Miller's Bible College and Institution values individual development, open communication and trust. However, managers are there to achieve results, and to do this primarily through coordination and synchronization people. But an overemphasis on the task people content of management diverts attention from the fact that in managing events, managers discovered that they have to be personally involved.

Michael Armstrong wrote

> Treating people right means treating them fairly well and with respect. To respect someone is to recognise a person quality, ensuring that they feel valued and treating them with dignity and courtesy - no belittling, no bullying. It means being sensitive to the differences between people, taking this diversity into account in any dealings with them. 76

There is a growing body of literature which describes the experiences of different organisation included church, school, business, etc., which have started their journey to become a learning organisation. Some of the most critical skills you can have as employee are organizational abilities / organizational skills. They're the skills you need to make sure you don't fall behind on your work. Organizational skills are one of the most sought-after employment skills, since they are critical to effective planning, time management, and prioritization efforts. Being organized will help us meet deadlines, reduce stress, and complete tasks more quickly. All produce qualitative and quantitative evidence to support their decisions and to identify positive changes in their organizational skills.

Mumford suggests that it is:

> Impossible to conceive of a learning organisation, however defined, which exists without individual learners. The learning organisation depends absolutely on the skills, approaches and commitment of individuals of their own learning. [77]

Furthermore, he contends that individuals are empowered to take control of their own personal destiny by being given opportunities to learn. If you want to take a pragmatic view of your organisation staff, regard them as an important investment. They cost money to acquire and maintain and they should provide a return on that basis outlay; their value increases as they become more effective in their tasks goals and capable of taking on greater responsibility. If the organisations help in the repositioning of HRM into a central strategic position, the concept is, without doubt, to be welcomed by personnel professionals. They're the many abilities needed to prioritize tasks, manage your time, and deliver results.

According to Holly McGurgan

> Developing good organizational skills, defined as the ability to efficiently manage your time, workload and resources, may help you improve your productivity and lower

your stress level. Your organizational abilities directly affect your ability to meet deadlines and produce thorough, high-quality work. [78]

Even Garratt voiced his worries about the possible problems that emerge with directors saying and doing different things:

> Paradoxically, top managers now mouth the words 'our people are our major asset', but do not behave as if this is so. [79]

This is just as true today, but to make the best use of experience it is helpful to place it in a framework that defines your understanding of what management is about, and helps you to reflect on and analyze your own experiences and the behaviour of others. There is also a wealth of knowledge about the skills that managers need to focus on and the aspects of managing people, including activities and themselves that they need to understand. None of these skills provides a quick efficiency improvement to our universally applicable. It is useful to know about them, but it is also necessary to develop an understanding of how they are best applied and modified to meet the particular requirements of the situation in which we find ourselves. Michael Armstrong mentioned that

> It is in your own interest and that of your organisation to enhance the skills and capabilities of the people you manage through coaching, training and importantly, giving them scope to learn or develop skills by providing new work opportunities or challenges. In doing so you will be treating them right. [80]

No matter what organization we work in or what role we perform, organizational skills are highly sought after by employers. Being able to prioritize, plan, and effectively manage one's time are all transferable skills that increase the efficiency of any business. With strong organizational skills, unforeseen issues are less daunting, and plans are in place for every eventuality. While every employee has a different organizational style, some organizational skills are important across the board.

Organizational Skills
Organizational skills are all about being able to prioritize tasks, maximize efficiency, and maintain structure throughout a workday or a project's lifespan. Discipline, cognitive flexibility, and memory are all crucial to being a strong organizer. Organizational skills are essential for any organization's long-term success. This encourages individuals in habits compatible with the notion of lifelong learning. It is therefore no surprise that Kolb addresses his ideas to managers and suggests that experiential learning will enable managers to cope with changes and complexity. He has suggested that:

> A key function of strategic management development....is to provide managers with access to knowledge and relationship networks that can help them become like long learners and cope with the issues on their continually changing agendas. [81]

At such time individuals are asked to 'reflect' upon their learning experiences. The reflective process demands they place themselves central stage and it reinforce the circular process of organisational skills. It does not see skills as the end result, as some kind of 'product ' but as an ongoing process, which never finishes. It leads to individuals redefining their current perspectives to develop new skills of thinking and behaving. Management is a process that exists to get results by making the best use of the human, financial and material resources available to the organisation and to individual managers. The overall process of management is subdivided into a number of individual processes that are required methods of operation specially designed to assist in the Organisation achievement of objectives. Without them, for Miller's Bible College and Institution can lose both time and money, and find it difficult to operate in a smooth manner. According to Laurie Mullins

> Creativity draws crucially on our ordinary abilities.
> Noticing remembering, seeing, speaking, hearing, understanding, language and recognizing analysis; all these talents of everyman are important. [82]

Organizational skills are those that enable one to make efficient and effective use of our resources. Being organized means we can effectively manage our time, energy, and workplace and complete all of our allocated duties. "Organizational skills" is a large category that includes several other types of skills. For example, project planning, mental organization, teamwork, and physical organization! Depending on our industry and job title, organizational skills can take many forms, but they usually entail keeping a clean workspace, managing deadlines, and communicating effectively with our coworkers.

According to Michael Armstrong

> Essentially, management is about deciding
> what to do and then getting it done through
> people. This definition emphasises that
> people are the most important resource
> available to managers. It is through this
> resource that all other resources - processes
> and systems knowledge, finance, materials,
> plant, equipment, etc., - will be managed. [83]

Good organizational skills help to create structure and order
in our life. Without organization, our life can dissolve into
chaos and confusion. Organizational abilities make us feel
less stressed because we have taken the steps necessary
to manage what is controllable in our life. Like when
staffs at Miller's Bible College and Institution performing
professional duties, interviewing for a job or students,
or conducting basic lifestyle chores, it is important to
demonstrate our organizational skills. Staying organized
is important for any student to be successful. One of the
lessons from Allan P. Miller, lack of organization is the
leading barrier to student success.

Allan P. Miller has given this useful advice:

> Think in an organized manner. For some, it's
> an issue of getting started and for others it's
> difficult maintaining an organization system.
> Organizational skills, but also for students
> apply to any age. It's never too late to practice
> organization in the classroom. We cannot
> become an organized person unless our frame

of mind is structured accordingly. We have to develop the balanced mind state necessary to put these tasks into action. If our mind is chaotic, pinpoint the source and work on eliminating it so we can have the calculating state of mind we need to be organized. [84]

It may seem obvious, but sorting alleviates disorganization so that papers and documents aren't misplaced. Sorting school work into binders and folders is a practical skill to teach students. This skill not only teaches students organisational skills but also how to prioritize items. With strong organisational skills, deadlines are never a cause for concern; just another factor in determining which tasks get done first. Knowing what tasks require immediate attention and which can be delayed, and for how long, is crucial to proper time management. With strong skills in time management, we'll never felt overwhelmed by our workload, because we know exactly which tasks have priority. They are able to recognize when an assignment needs to be dealt with immediately, and when other tasks need to be given precedence. Our strong organizational skills help to ensure that we know how to manage our time. They enable us to make the right kinds of plans and execute them in the most efficient manner possible.

Principles of Management Skills
Management is a generic term and subject to many interpretations. A number of different ideas are attributed to the meaning of management and to the work of a manager. In certain respects everyone could be regarded as a manager to some extent. However, we are concerned with management as involving people looking beyond

themselves and exercising formal authority over the activities and performance of other people.

> At its most basic, management may be viewed as 'making things happen'. Management is active, not theoretical. It is about changing behaviour and making things happen. It is about developing people, working with them, reaching objectives and achieving results. Indeed, all the research into how managers spend their time reveals that they are creatures of the moment, perpetually immersed in the nitty-gritty of making things happen. [85]

Whilst the accountability process is by no means restricted to the public sector environment, it must be accepted that the public sector provides an excellent illustration of both the need for and exercise of such a process. Hence in this chapter examines ways in which crises may arise in the workplace. Three different scenarios are presented for study. They cover a range of situations that present different challenges and highlight how crises may vary in their potential impact on organisations and individual managers. This is intended to facilitate effective implementation of learning.

The English Dictionary defines management as: (n).
> The process of managing or being managed; the action of managing. The professional administration of business concerns, public undertakings, etc. people engaged in this. The governing body; the board of directors or the people in charge of running a business, regarded collectively. [86]

According to this dictionary study, management is tasks. Management is discipline. Management is also people. Every achievement of management is the achievement of a manager. Every failure is a failure of a manger. The problem is identifying a single discipline which encompasses the work of a manger, or agreeing the disciplines that a manager needs in order effectively to carry out this work.

The accountability process can be viewed from the perspective of the organisation itself or from the perspective of individuals within the organisation. That is the organisation itself will be accountable for its policies and actions and individuals within the organisation will be accountable for their performance. Even within a work organisation you cannot identify a manager necessarily by what a person is called or by his or her job title. As a result there are a number of peoples whose job title includes, the term manager but who, in reality, are not performing the full activities of a manager. This involves agreeing the outcomes required, planning work activities to deliver these outcomes and the monitoring activities to make sure service standards and legal requirements have been met. This includes a 'process for working through' and systematic approaches applicable to aspects of managing crises or activities, with relevant reading.

a. Identify what you anticipate might be common or potential situation that could arise in your own organisation, based on your knowledge and past experience of it or similar organisations. As with all such rules there are exceptions, since the ability to influence the environment tends to increase with the size of the firm. Even if there are certain innate qualities which makes for a potentially good manager, these natural talents must be encouraged and developed through proper guidance, education and training, and planned experience. Clearly, management must always be something of an art, especially in so far as it involves practice, personal judgement and dealing with people. However, it still requires knowledge of the fundamentals of management, and competence in the application of specific skills and techniques – as illustrated, for example, with developments in information technology.

Firstly, from the organisational perspective, other people have given the organisation money; it is necessary therefore in the economic exchange for the organisation to account for the spending of that money. This it can do by delivering (to that person's satisfaction) the good or service for which the money was paid. Thus, in many ways, the customer can be seen to be a very active participant in the accountability process. Similarly, from the individual perspective, the individual employee is financially rewarded by the organisation and as such the organisation can reasonably expect to hold him or her accountable for his or her actions.

Dr. David Needle wrote:

> There are a variety of ways in which economic changes have affected businesses in this country. We will illustrate these changes through the changing nature of world economies, including structural changes, the supply and price of raw materials, increasing international competition and the emergence of the multinational as a powerful influence. The case of the multinational illustrates

the difficulty of isolating business and environmental influences. Many businesses in this country have undoubtedly been influenced by a world economy increasingly dominated by multinational corporations. These same multinationals are themselves businesses with the ability to influence national and international economies. [87]

Secondly, we define the environment as comprising all factors which exist outside the business enterprise, but which interact with it. As I point out in the dictionary, definitions tend to see the two words as synonymous. Management is sometimes referred to as 'administration of business concerns' and administration as 'management of public affairs'. There is clearly an overlap between the two terms and they tend to be used, therefore, in accordance with the convenience of individual writers. All firms are to a greater or lesser extent constrained by the environment within which they operate, but the activities of businesses themselves also change that same environment.

b. Identify what personal – work interface activities could theoretically arise for you, at some point in the future, that could have an impact on you and your organisation. Political factors – even though the points made previously are legitimate, it must be accepted that it is a political reality that the democratic process itself would demand accountability in the public service if the previously mentioned points did not exist.

Thus it is difficult to envisage a situation where elections were completely abolished no matter how competitive the environment within which public service organisations works.

L. J. Mullins wrote:

> Administration can be seen as taking place in accordance with some form of rules or procedures, whereas management implies a greater degree of discretion. For our purposes, management is viewed as applying to both private and public sector organisations; and administration is interpreted as part of the management process, and concerned with the design and implementation of systems and procedures to help meet stated objectives. Systems of communication and procedures relating to information technology are particularly important today. [88]

More helpful – and challenging – however, is to highlight those that are not part of the routine at one's own organisation, and to consider including them. Even if a list of leadership qualities could be identified, the qualities approach does not form the best starting point for leadership training. It is often associated with the view that leaders are born and not made. Yes, all leadership qualities can be developed – some more than others – by practice and experience.

The goal: to use this new understanding of best practices to put the entire enterprise of improving "soft skills" on a sounder, more scientific footing. These guidelines offer to improve work activities, we need to monitor activities, trends and developments and invite others to come forward with their suggestions for improvements. Dealings with people from other cultures we must recognize that differences do exist and be prepared to adjust behaviour and expectations accordingly. This is the theme of many recent initiatives in training for international management.

We need to plan the change, check people's understanding and commitment to the change and monitor the implementation of our plans to ensure the intended improvements are achieved. We also need to ensure that work quality is maintained to an acceptable standard during the period of change. It will also increase your potential for its effective implementation in and application to your own work as a manager.

1. I ensure the agree requirements with my clients in sufficient detail to allow work to be planned effectively.
2. I plan with my teams to allow requirements to be met within agreed time scales.
3. I explain plans to all the relevant team members in sufficient detail and at an appropriate level and pace.
4. I do confirm with my team members their understanding, and commitment to the plans in writing following by a phone call.
5. I gave opportunities to all team members to make recommendations for improving plans for a better service, which I record.

Such a systematic, objective method is needed to get a true picture of the competences that matter most for a given role. For instance, a manager who tries to shift his or her leadership style may also need to improve in self-awareness in order to make the other change.

David said:

> While convergence as an idea represents a somewhat superficial analysis, we have seen that, its practical implications are that because industrialized societies are moving in the same direction, we may therefore learn from the mistakes of others further along the route. We have seen also that the supporters of the 'culture specific' hypothesis believe that specific aspects of business are especially susceptible to cultural and national influences. [89]

I believe what Dr. David Needle is saying, the useful ideas and methods may be transplanted but care must be taken to see that they have been adapted to the new cultural setting and that there is an understanding of the supporting conditions needed for their development. The fundamental problem of management is that organisational and individual objectives differ. Whereas the organisation may be interested in maximising output and minimising cost, the individual employee may have other priorities. The problem for the organisation is how to eliminate opportunism. One must ensure that the following:

a. Opportunities to relevant people to make recommendations for improvements to work activities.

b. Plans are presented for improvements to relevant people at an appropriate time.
c. You confirm relevant people's understanding of the change and their commitment to their role in it, including identifying any resistance to the change.
d. Results of the change are reported to relevant people in the agreed format and timescale.

It is good to keep in mind the following:

1. Your monitoring of activities occurs at intervals most likely to identify potential improvements.
2. Your monitoring of the change is sufficient to ensure the intended improvements are achieved.

Time Management Skills
Our mastery of time management is a reflection on our overall professionalism and management expertise. Having a realistic sense of time as well as applying tools that will keep us on track with our schedule demonstrates our time management skills. Effective time management can help us feel more fulfilled and can set a positive example for our coworkers and employees to follow. Christian Fisher has made this point on schedule about what really matters:

> Allocate blocks of time for all of the important matters you need to focus on to have a balanced daily life. In addition to time for work, scheduling time for other priorities such as spouse, kids, friends, volunteering, exercise or hobbies is also important. Calculate the time you want or need to spend on your important priorities each day. [90]

Accept that we can't do all things all of the time, and attempting that will make effective time management virtually impossible. Be decisive in eliminating tasks and activities that take up more of our time than they're worth or that distract us from our more important goals. Being organized requires good time management skills. Allowing ourselves adequate time to complete chores, avoiding spending too much time on any one activity, and balancing our time at home and at work are all examples of time management. Time management is critical since it allows one to preserve energy and remain calm in a fast-paced setting. The point of a deadline is to keep tasks, deliverables, and projects under control so that business operations can flow smoothly. In retail or restaurant jobs, time management is crucial for serving customers promptly and keeping them pacified even when it is busy. Time management is an important skill employers look for because without it, a business can lose clients, miss goals, fail in efficiency, or miss important time specific opportunities.

According to Holly McHurgan:

> A block system can help you chart how time you actually spend on tasks, allowing you to make changes that help you work more efficiently. Although it's a good idea to organize tasks by their importance, spending too much time on one subject can be tiring and may lead to mistakes. You may benefit by incorporating short breaks into your schedule. [91]

Time management requires a good sense of work gauge so that you can correctly allot the time needed for a task. But it's not just about scheduling. Good time management also requires discipline, quick thinking, knowing how and when to delegate, and knowing when to use strategies for dealing with procrastination, distraction, and even unplanned events. A crucial aspect of office organizing is deciding when and how to utilize our time. A person with great time management skills can adapt to new problems and readjust as needed to complete an assignment. This combination of planning, scheduling, strategy, delegation, and adaptability are the kinds of traits that make an employee dependable, and employers look out for that. Being able to prioritize our numerous tasks is a crucial aspect of mental organizing. Breaking down multi-step procedures into their constituent parts and determining the best sequence to execute them demonstrates our problem-solving abilities.

Making the most of our time and energy, as well as minimizing stress for us and our team, is the goal of prioritizing. It doesn't matter if we cross three items off our to do list before noon; if we don't getting things done the most essential item checked off, we're not prioritizing appropriately. In addition, well organized individuals often get a good night's sleep, plan the week ahead, search for useful tools that save time, and communicate using sensible strategies in an efficient manner.

Scott Morgan has given this useful advice:

> Make plans, set deadlines and stick to your schedules. This allows you to focus your time and energy on the bigger items first, rather than getting bogged down in minutia. Checklists also serve as a reminder to do things by a

certain day or time, thus eliminating surprises
– at inconvenient times. ₉₂

Good time management means being able to schedule the right tasks for the right time frames, which leads to things getting done sooner. It's also about eliminating distractions of the unforeseen issues such as weather-related power outages may not be our fault, but we will pay the price if our work is late because of them. Develop a system for completing individual tasks in chunks, before their due dates.

Listening Skills
Listening is one of the most important skills we can have. How well we listen has a major impact on our job effectiveness, and on the quality of our relationships with others. Clearly, listening is a skill that we can all benefit from improving. By become a better listener we can improve our productivity, as well as our ability to influence, persuade and negotiate. Listing specific examples of practicing organizational skills will provide the hiring manager with a greater sense of what we can offer. For example, as an administrative assistant, ensuring that office materials are in their proper place. Listening isn't a passive activity, but a process that you actively undertake. To be a better listener, you must be focused on the speaker, their message, and let the speaker know you understand what's been said.

When deciding how to satisfy the needs we should remember that it is not just about selecting suitable training courses. Personal development planning aims to promote learning and to provide us with knowledge and a portfolio of transferable skills that will help to progress our career.

We convey our confidence negative ones can undermine it and need to be dealt with. Confidence was defined by Rob Yeung as:

> To be confident is to be self-assured with a firm belief in one's capacity to get things done well. The ability takes appropriate and effective action, however, challenging it may appear at the time. Confident people are positive about what they do and optimistic about their ability to deal with the situations they face. [93]

Convey our confidence to others by speaking out and varying types of skills pace pitch and emphasis on our intelligence abilities. I am saying that to be succeed it is not enough to have technical ability and a high intelligence quotient; emotional intelligence is also required. Someone with lots of technical, professional or specialist expertise is promoted to a managerial job and fails. This may be partly attributed to an inability to manage in the sense of planning, organizing and controlling the use of resources.

In other words, an inadequate level of emotional intelligence is what Daniel Goleman pointed out:

> Self-awareness is the ability to recognise and understand your moods, emotions and drives as well as their effect on others. This is linked to three competences: self-confidence, realistic self-assessment and emotional self-awareness. Social awareness- the ability to understand the emotional makeup of others

people and skills in treating people according
to their emotional reactions. 94

Clear thinking is logical thinking. It is useful process for reasoning by which one judgement is derived from another and correct conclusions are drawn from the evidence. If we say that people are logical, we mean that they draw reasonable inferences to their conclusions can be proved by reference to the organisation facts used to support them.

According to Michael Armstrong wrote:

> Here are some comments on coping with a reverse in your fortunes:
> 1. Learn from what has happened
> 2. If you have made mistakes, analysis how and why you did and how you can avoid making it again.
> 3. Asses your strength and work out how you can use them more effectively in the future.
> 4. Asses your weakness and what you need to do to overcome them.
> 5. Seek the views of those you respect on what action you should take. 95

Things can go wrong through events beyond our control or through incompetence. It is difficult and very rare for anyone to admit that they are incompetent, but this is why things most frequently go adrift. It is therefore useful to know that good managers are decisive. They can quickly size up a situation and reach the right conclusion on what should be done about it. A complicated situation can often be resolved by separating the whole into its component parts. Even if we have discussed the fact first, some people will probably look for those facts that fit the conclusion they have already reached. We have to think carefully not only about how things are to be achieved or done, but also about its impact on the people concerned and the extent to which they will cooperate.

Michael Armstrong wrote:

> If you pick up the wrong person for the job they will underperform and make mistakes. You must ensure that you specify exactly what you want in terms of experience, qualifications, knowledge, skills and personality, and that you do not settle for second best. [96]

The way to improve our listening skills is to practice active listening. Making and maintaining eye contact with the speaker lets them know they have your undivided attention. This is where we make a conscious effort to hear not only the words that another person is saying but, more importantly, the complete message being communicated. Listen without judging the other person or mentally criticizing the things she tells you. If the speaker's message is unclear, ask clarifying questions to gain more information. You can also ask confirming questions, such as "I want to make sure I got that right. It sounds like you're saying is that correct?" This can help you gauge if you've received the message accurately. If you're engaged with a teacher, colleague, or manager, take notes and leave room for silence. This allows you to take a beat and process the information you've received before asking for more information.

There are numerous benefits associated with being a good listener. People with refined listening skills can help others feel secure in expressing their opinions. They may also be better able to reduce tension during arguments and communicate respect to the speaker. Other potential benefits include being more likable, building stronger relationships, and having a clearer understanding of what's being discussed. Deep listening occurs when you're committed to understanding the speaker's perspective. It involves paying attention to both verbal and nonverbal cues, such as the words being used, the speaker's body language, and their tone. This type of listening helps build trust and rapport, and it helps others feel comfortable in expressing their thoughts and opinions.

Listen without jumping to conclusions. Remember that the speaker is using language to represent the thoughts and feelings inside her brain. You don't know what those thoughts and feelings are and the only way you'll find out is by listening. Now that you've made eye contact, relax. You don't have to stare fixedly at the other person. You can look away now and then and carry on like a normal person. The important thing is to be attentive. Critical listening involves using systematic reasoning and careful thought to analyze a speaker's message and separate fact from opinion. Critical listening is often useful in situations when speakers may have a certain agenda or goal, such as watching political debates, or when a salesperson is pitching a product or service.

Allow your mind to create a mental model of the information being communicated. Whether a literal picture, or an arrangement of abstract concepts, your brain will do the necessary work if you stay focused, with senses fully alert. When listening for long stretches, concentrate on, and remember, key words and phrases. Mentally screen out distractions, like background activity and noise. In addition, try not to focus on the speaker's accent or speech mannerisms to the point where they become distractions. Finally, don't be distracted by your own thoughts, feelings, or biases.

Physical Organizational Skills
This is probably the organizational skill that first springs to mind when one thinks about organization. Keeping our workspace free from clutter, appropriate filling / record keeping, and managing our physical resources efficiently are all elements of physical organizational skills. Physical organization includes not just a tidy desk, but also the layout of rooms, floors, and whole buildings, also students in studies, and it goes well beyond maintaining a neat appearance. Sometimes keeping our work space - whether that's our desk, restaurant kitchen, or desktop computer - neat and functional is another important organizational skill. Clutter all over our desk spells coming trouble. It's just a matter of time before items get misplaced, lost, or accidentally damaged. Examples of physical organization skills are keeping track of items as they're used, returning items to their places after use, and creating and developing sensible strategies and physical solutions for facilitating work flow, cleanliness, and efficiency in a work space.

Basically, we are seeking to provide control two areas - input and output - and the team relationships between them, which is productivity or performance. It is about moving on to a new or future state that has been defined generally in terms of strategic planning, vision and scope. It will cover the purpose and mission of the organisation team, its corporate philosophy on such matters as growth, quality, innovation and values concerning people, the customer needs served and the technologies employed.

Rosabeth Moss Kanter wrote

> The process starts with an awareness of the need for change. Possible courses of action can then be identified and evaluated and a choice made of the preferred action. It is then necessary to decide how to get from here to there. It is here that the problems of introducing change emerge and have to be managed. 97

This concept of splitting the difference is essentially pessimistic. An alternative or attempt is made to ensure that a reasonable solution to the problem rather than just accommodating different points of view. This is where the apparent paradox of creative conflict comes in.

Michael Armstrong wrote

> The process of dealing with a pressurized situation in a way that plans, organises, directs and controls a number of interrelated operations and guides the decision-making process of those in charge to a rapid but unhurried resolution of the acute problem faced by the organisation. 98

If we can also foresee potential issues and create solutions for them ahead of time, we're showcasing our strategic abilities. Prioritizing is about making the most of our time and energy, and reducing stress for you and our team throughout a project's lifespan. Other resources studies have also shown links between personality and learning skills and have found for example that. Such studies highlight the necessary skills for trainers to be sensitive not only to the organisation personality but also to be aware of the impact their own interest and experience. So, given the complexity of learning how can managers make sense of the theories, concepts and framework? The importance of creativity as a management ability has been creeping into the management educational agenda over the past decade lending a so-called soft edge to the business literature. For organisations to be innovative, creative solutions are required. Such a statement is in total harmony with the research on organizational skills.

West could be speaking about organisations when he says:

> Organisations and teams which practices reflexivity and are prepared to continually challenge.... The better anticipate and manage problems, and they deal with conflict as a valuable process asset within the organisation, encouraging effectiveness, growth and development... The most reflexive organisations are those within which there is a maelstrom of activity, debate, arguments, innovation and a real sense of involvement of all employees. [99]

Material is more easily learned when it is associated and organized in as many ways as possible. Using resources effectively (times, libraries, tutorials etc.) is self-evident, essential, but frequently forgotten. Constantly testing your knowledgeable skills and reviewing materials are also good practice. But being positive, getting rid of anxiety and emotional factors, may be the most difficult, but is probably the most important part of this presentation process of organisational skills. The growth of any society requires individuals to develop new skills and competences and to have a flexible attitude to cope with future challenges. There are factors that managers need to focus on to influence in order to improve the quality of effectiveness of the organisation. As Wilson, pointed out, for example, although teamworking, like most management ideas, is very simple nevertheless this simplicity conceals a great challenge.

Wilson wrote:

> The principles of teamworking may be easily understood, but the task of installing it can be quite daunting. Introducing teamworking is not a straightforward grafting job, the simple matter of adding a new idea to those already in place. Every teamworking application is different. Each organisation, department and individual group is faced with unique problems and in some situations, it is more about getting rid of old ways of doing things than infecting new ones. [100]

Organisational performance and the satisfaction derived by assessing individuals are influenced by the interactions among other members of the group. Members of a group must work well together as a team and there must be a good spirit of unity and cooperation. However, this is not meaning to be evasive, but assuming that there is a number of important dependences and acknowledges that. Vecchio also refers to the contingency approach as it depends.

> The difficult of offering simple general principles to explain or predict behaviour in Organisational setting.... If you ask a contingency researcher for a simple answer to a seemingly simple question, you should expect to be given a fairly complex and highly qualified answer. Because human behaviour is itself complex, a statement of behavioural principles must also be complex. [101]

The nature of work and studies at Miller's Bible College and Institution is being redefined and this has created strong pressures for greater flexibility in patterns of work organisation and in the education sector in the twenty-first century. Empowerment makes greater use of the knowledge, skills, and abilities of the organisational workforce; it encourages teamworking; and if there is meaningful participation, it can aid the successful implementation of change programmers. It requires thinkers and doers to work closely together. Top management team must create a climate in which managers have the scope to develop new skills, ideas and the ideas resources to help implement them. This will include reviewing performance against agreed plans, and assessing competence requirements and your capacity to achieve them. The analysis is required methods therefore based on an understanding of what we're expected to do, the knowledge and skills we need to carry out our job effectively, what we have achieved, and what knowledge and skills we have. If there are any gaps between the knowledge and skills we need and those we have, then this defines a development need.

Michael Armstrong wrote:

> The analysis is always related to work and the capacity to carry it out effectively. By making your own assessment of your personal development needs a basis for identifying the means of satisfying them and acting accordingly, you can get more satisfaction from your work, advance your career and increase your employability. [102]

Chapter Six

The Importance of Teamwork in the Organisational Setting

Characteristics of Team

Team building is the process of deliberately creating an effective team by focusing on those factors that support team performance. Common team building activities focus on clarifying roles and goals; building trust, accountability and commitment, improvising or designing processes; supporting the use of healthy team norms to encourage effective communication and conflict management. Team building can make groups to effectively work together to accomplish organisational goals for many years. The issue here is not making choices, but making choices that are based on principles that are set forth in the best interest of the organisation. None of the choices are intrinsically right or wrong. If the choice is to build the teams within the current departments it will be relatively easy to get some quick efficiency improvements. Each person knows the work of the department and can probably offer good suggestions for improving the way work is done.

Kenneth O. Gangel wrote:

> Teams, we see them all the time. We root for – or against them. We function in them, both in the family and in the workplace. We watch them

on TV teams, or groups of dissimilar people, bonding together. In that bonding, they face enemies without and conflicts within. Depending on the circumstances, differing members of the team may take starring or lead roles. [103]

This elevation of teams, personal bonding, and leadership by gift hardly represents a new theme in literature or art. Nevertheless, the emphasis on individual student at Miller's Bible College and Institution by trying and ensuring that sessions on studies flows progressively, that is, it is delivered in a logical order and stresses progress continually and are approachable to all. My research on "team work" has revealed that team work can be effective in an environment where everyone has an opportunity to fully participate and add to the growing body literature. It has involved directly in education; this means everyone has the same opportunity; there are no boundaries such as ethnicity, gender or disability. During that time all the individual's feel valued, be able to mix and participate with all members of the group be in a safe and positive environment.

George Weber has emphasized that "the historic command structure organisation is dead" and reminds us that:

> The successful leader of the future must have one more attribute that weights perhaps as much as all the others on the scale of effectiveness; he or she must be a tireless, inventive, observant, risk-taking, and ever-hopeful builder and enabler of management and leadership teams within and among the organisation's constituent parts. [104]

This shift, as we approach the end of the century, is one problem continues and perhaps even magnifies itself in our organisational vacuum all around us; and this is the "importance of teamwork". In these policies and procedures of promoting teamwork and organisational positive behaviour in education literatures, I have tried to make my research has also revealed that, in a strong and healthy team, every individual feels valued. They are able to mix and participate with all other members of the group, in a safe and positive environment speaking to groups directly, using eye contact, addressing them by their names; asking them direct questions. Initially, I carry out an assessment to test their prior knowledge on individual basis, their preferred learning styles and to assess if any additional support is required by. I then adjust the studies level and pitch it correctly to each individual. Equality ensures individuals or groups of individuals are treated fairly and equally (Equality Act 2010 and the Equality Act 2020) No less favourably, specific to their needs, including areas of race, gender, disability, religion or belief, sexual orientation and age. Diversity aims to recognise, respect and value people's differences to contribute and realise their full potential by promoting an inclusive culture for all individuals.

We have had ample opportunity to study its alleged irrelevance, tradition bound immobility, and inability to meet the needs of modern society. Some of the criticism was deserved and much of it, helpful. Nevertheless, one basic erroneous note flowed through most of the literature dissecting the organisation during those decades. But what I am now studying reflects some fuzzy thinking that has been hanging around the corners of my mind for a long time, thinking that has recently climbed to centre stage and gained a compellingly clear focus. After a quarter century of puzzling over people's problems and wondering how different organisation of psychologist could help, I have been captured by an idea that is moving me away from familiar ground toward large fields of uncharted territory.

Larry Crabb has written about this idea; he said:

> Ordinary people have the power to change other people live. The power is found in connection, that profound meeting when the truest part of one soul meets the emptiest recesses in another and finds something there, when life passes from one to the other. When that happens, the giver is left fuller than before and the receiver less terrified, eventually eager, to experience even deeper, more mutual connection. 105

I have come to believe that the root of all our personal and emotional difficulties is a lack of togetherness a failure to connect that keeps us from receiving life and prevents the life in us from spilling over onto others. However, the concept and use of teams as a central element of decision making and performances are more recent. The whole idea of the team is to get as many different ideas about a given problem or opportunity. A task team needs multiple perspectives to realise its potential, but it does not need people who are unable to learn or to see the value in another point of view. Throughout the study I have attempted to make use of both secular and Christian leadership literature. These are all important and I have taken them into consideration throughout the study.

The successful use of teams is also at the cornerstone of management in many Bible Colleges, including Miller's Bible College and Institution, organisations where teams are used as planning tools and as the key to quality student care. Teams made up of not only internal staff but also external consultants have been central in the successful performance of candidates of the institution. The bases for effective use of teams are the same in the private and public sectors. Each of the three kinds of teams has very different needs and Implications; and if the organisation is going to develop effective teams, it must address the differences within and among these teams. One of the most celebrated examples of the use of teams is the one that Larry Osborne talks about.

> This team building has had a significant impact on our business meetings. I can't remember the last time we had an honest to goodness argument. [106]

The first distinguishing characteristic of a team is its members remain faithful to a common goal and have often developed themselves. Members must learn to accept and agree that the team goal is worthwhile and agree on a general approach to that goal. Such agreement provides the vision and motivation for team members to perform. The success of the team depends on a number of key factors. First, the members of a team have to be selected carefully for their complementary skills and expertise like what Harold Longenecker talks about. He wrote:

> Servant leaders are not just there, waiting to be picked. They require a suitable climate in which to grow and mature, and it is the

task of Christian leaders to help create that climate. [107]

The second characteristic is mutual accountability. To succeed as a team, members must feel and be accountable to one another and to the organisation for the process and outcome of their work. Whereas group members report to the leader or manager and are accountable to them, team members take on responsibility and perform because of their commitment to the team. Second, the team members need to focus on and be committed to the team goal. For example, individuals from different functional departments such as marketing or production, although selected because of their expertise in particular areas, need to leave the department mind set behind and focus on the task of the team.

The third characteristic of a team is a team culture based on trust and collaboration. Whereas group members share norms, team members have a shared culture. Team members are willing to compromise, Cooperate, and collaborate to reach their common purpose. Third, the team task has to be appropriately complex and the team has to be provided with the critical capabilities and resources it needs to perform the task. Thus, management teams must take on tasks that inspire and integrate the work of the expense of the organisation. This work usually comes in the form of building a vision, refining the culture, carrying out major change initiatives, or improving the moral image of the organisation or unit.

Why Organisations Have Teams
The purpose of creating teams is to provide a framework that will increase the ability of employees to participate in

planning, problem-solving, and decision-making to better serve customers. Many times, when you're hired or promoted into a leadership role, the team is already there. You have to adapt your ideas and plans to fit the knowledge, skills, and abilities of the existing team. This was a purpose the task force members could rally around because the company's quality-based brand was indeed at stake and that affected everyone. Finding the real purpose lifted the whole effort above the level of parochial interests. Teamwork is when two or more people work together to complete a certain task. The members of the team may have different tasks, but they cooperate together and work toward the same goal. Some activities require teamwork, such as team sports. Teamwork is especially useful when the team consists of people with different skill sets. Finding or confirming the real purpose of any group, permanent or temporary, is the first step you must take as its leader. If you don't, there's a good chance the group will never come together to work as a collective whole, a team. Its work in total will likely be less than the sum of individual efforts because members will duplicate work, pursue their own interests, or even labour at counter-purposes.

Belbin describes team role as a pattern of behaviour, characteristic of the way in which one team member interacts with another where performance serves to facilitate the progress of the team as a whole. Blbin's eight key team roles are:

> Company worker
> Chairman
> Shaper
> Plant
> Resource Investigator

Monitor Evaluator
Team Worker
Completer Finisher. [108]

The eight types of people identified are useful team members and form a comprehensive list. In fact, teams and team thinking have been around for years. Being a student at Miller's Bible College and Institution, one of roles is to identifying and meeting the needs of my studies that boosts my morale and encourage me. It is essential that I understand that important the world is facing severe challenges and needs people to undertake the challenges – people from different backgrounds, ideals, beliefs, abilities and ways of thinking. It requires an inclusive learning, teaching and research attitude and culture to enable students, staff and stakeholders to develop their full potential and ultimately contribute to the challenges of this day. But sometimes, you get to create your own team. It can happen on special projects when you're pulling people from different departments, or when you are creating a new department.

If you're in the situation where you get to create a team from scratch here's how to create the best team possible. No wonder collective purpose is the first requirement in creating any real team. Not just any lofty-sounding purpose will work, however. "To be the best," "to have the highest quality," "to be the most trusted" — unless they're backed up with genuine research and evidence and ongoing effort — rarely generate much excitement. To provide meaning, a purpose must be real, tangible, and compelling. Adding more people with the same skills to a task does not necessarily help the team complete the task any sooner. However, time efficiency is not the only benefit to using teamwork to complete a task. Quality of work increases because people on teams have more accountability. They also have teammates to help catch mistakes and people from which to learn new skills. Teamwork also increases morale, especially when teammates are able to celebrate achievements together. Once you get your team together, you've got to run it. Great teams seldom run well without a great leader. Only that's they are doing something job. Make sure that you work to make the team cohesive and hard working. Don't ask more of them than you ask of yourself.

Organisations are much more likely to perform well when their people work effectively as a team. This is because good teamwork creates synergy – where the combined effect of the team is greater than the sum of individual efforts. Working together a team can apply individual perspectives, experience, and skills to solve complex problems, creating new solutions and ideas that may be beyond the scope of any one individual. Purpose also needs to be made tangible and kept vital through concrete goals and plans. To create a team capable of extraordinary collective work, team members need to know not only that they do something important (purpose) but also that they are going someplace worthwhile and challenging (goals and plans). Teams and teamwork are not novel concepts. In fact, teams and team thinking have been around for years at companies such as the need to identify the soft skills as well as the hard skills you need. Will the employee need to communicate results and progress to senior management? Are there skills you only that they are doing something going to be obvious without hard thought? For instance, if you're putting together a team to implement a new software system, you obviously need programmers.

Being inclusive within this context also requires understanding, preparedness and resources. These can enable college organisations to deal with an increasingly diverse set of student backgrounds, ability and attainment and larger classes whilst endeavouring to provide an excellent learning experience. Managers have discovered the large body of research indicating that teams can be more effective than the traditional corporate hierarchical structure for making decisions quickly and efficiently. Even simple changes like encouraging input and feedback from workers on the line can make a dramatic improvement.

The first has to do with specialisation. As the economy expands and organisations grow accordingly, firms become ever more complex, both in their tasks and in the markets they serve. Thus, the activities of individuals in these firms are necessarily becoming more specialised. These new relationships require team members to learn how to work with others to achieve their goals. Team members must integrate through coordination and synchronisation with suppliers, managers, peers, and customers. It's more important for me to ensure learning is taking place with my students than to keep to my timings.

The benefits include:

a. I can connect and engage with a variety of individuals
b. The social and ethical impact on the way the Miller's Bible College and Institution staff and student community work creates a positive atmosphere of support for all its members.

The second challenge has to do with competition. In today's economy, a few large firms are emerging as dominant players in the biggest markets. These industry leaders often enjoy vast economies of scale and earn tremendous profits. Thus, bringing out the best in individuals within the firm has become ever more important. This means that people can be expected to specialise more and more in their areas of expertise and these areas of expertise will get ever narrower and more interdependent. On this foundation can then be built most everything else a team needs to work well — clarity about roles and responsibilities, agreed work processes, mutual values and expectations that shape interactions among members, and the means for ongoing performance assessment. In addition, they shape and guide the network of relationships you create with others throughout the broader organization. But you also need a person who can talk to the end-users to get a clear understanding of their true needs. You need a trainer who understands the technical side of the new software system and can explain it to non-techy people.

How about the people for whom you're responsible? Are they a cohesive team that's working collectively at the highest level they're capable of achieving? If not, look first at the purpose you're all pursuing. Are you solving a technical problem or restoring the company's reputation for quality? Are you saving and building an internal team over which you have advantages and disadvantages? The advantages are that you already know the people from whom you are choosing. You know their strengths and their weaknesses. You know who is good at technical work. You know who is creative. You know who is whiny. As well as enhancing organisation's performance good teamwork benefits individuals too. It enables mutual support and learning, and can generate a sense of belonging and commitment. The disadvantages are that you've got to pull the team from your existing staff, so you can't fix any weaknesses that already exist in your potential team members. You have to deal with the politics of pulling someone from another group's staff. You can't ignore the fact that you can damage relationships if you steal too many of the best people from other departments.

Additionally, you may know that John is the best possible person, but John has no interest in being on your team, or John's manager won't let him join. You may find pulling together an internal team super frustrating. The purpose of a team is the motivating force for why employees do what they do. Having direction in what their team is working toward can help individuals feel more encouraged to work and have a collective identity. Understanding ways to make a more purposeful team can help your organization attract and engage employees.

In this article, we discuss the purpose of a team, explain why it's important to know and provide a list of tips for making a more purposeful team. Start with your most senior person, or the person you want leading the team, and work down through the rest of the team members from this hire. You want your most senior person to help you with the additional hiring—either internally or externally.

Organisation Members Selection
The word organisation signifies "the process of choosing the most suitable candidate for the vacant position in the organization". In other words, selection means weeding out

unsuitable applicants and selecting those individuals with prerequisite qualifications and capabilities to fill the jobs in the organization. While the word organisation points to "the process of identifying and grouping the work to be performed, defining and delegating responsibility and authority, and establishing relationships for the purpose of enabling people to work most effectively together in accomplishing objectives." By understanding these learning techniques in our particular working environment is really important, some individual can be more productive in a very physical environment. Making an organization refers to a structure in which people come together to attain some common goals of selection. People feel that they can fulfill their needs more effectively when they become part of a group. In an organization, the individual goals are foregone for the group goals and the group goals are compromised for organizational goals so the maximum benefit can be derived by using limited available resources.

Invest some time in understanding the unique needs of each selection. In any course, there may be some overlap between the goals of a course and the personal goals of our selection. For example, a communications course should take into account the personal goals of a selection who seeks to improve their self-confidence in high-pressure communication scenarios, such as salary negotiations. An organization is influenced by many external and internal factors. External factors include politics, country's economy, and legal rules and regulations; whereas internal factors include plans, objectives, and policies of an organization. Internal factors can be controlled by an organization; however, external factors are beyond the organization's control.

Any organization activities are required for a variety of skills constant caution and adaptability to effectively manage situations arising due to such factors. Many benefits from learning in an environment where they feel included and where they are taught in ways that recognise and support their needs as individuals and as part of a learning community! By understanding these learning techniques in our particular working environment is really important, some individual can be more productive in a very physical environment. I use visual and hands on learning styles which suits a lot of selections, but not all. This is why there has to be open opportunities to suit all selections and we can evaluate this by asking people how they felt the learning is going and evaluating as we go along.

Organisation is the backbone of management because without an efficient organization no management can perform its functions smoothly in selection. In the management process this organization stands as a second state which tries to combine various activities in a business to accomplish pre-determined selection goals. It is the structural framework of duties and responsibilities required of personnel in performing various functions with a view to achieve business goals. Most group activities are required a variety of skills and knowledge. Given this requirement, it would be reasonable to consider be more likely to have diverse abilities and information and should be more effective.

Let us look at two resources that have received the greatest possible amount of attention which are: abilities and adjustment. Alike 'management' the term 'organization' has also been defined in a number of ways such as a process, as a structure of relationship, as a group of persons and as an open dynamic system and so on. Here we consider the same type of factors, but in a group context. That is, it is not whether a person is male or female or has been employed with the organisation a year rather than ten years that concerns us now, but rather the individual attribute in relation to the attributes of others with whom he or she works.

According to Craig Swenson

> If everyone is moderately dissimilar from everyone else in a group the feelings of being an outsider are reduced. [109]

The abilities to provide constructive feedback to my students to meet their individual needs could be like having handouts – this could help to support the visual students and the read / write students. It gives them reference points and allows them to take information away, read and digest it in their own time. This method also helps support individual needs by supporting my students with handouts before the course, so that dyslexic students may have a chance to read through so that they don't fall back during the class due to not having enough time to read and absorb the information. My handouts are of easy-to-read larger font and available in larger font more detailed handouts can also be given out for higher ability students without putting pressure on other students to keep up. More detailed I have at hand also Power Point presentation to use in class, if necessary.

First, evidence indicates that individuals, who hold crucial abilities for attending the organisation group task tend to be more involved in group activity, generally contribute towards more, are more likely to emerging as the group leaders, and are more satisfied if their talent are effectively utilized by the team. My students perform better when they know what exactly is expected of them. A part of a group performance can be predicted by assessing the task relevant and possible intellectual abilities of its individual members. Sure, the saying is true, that we saying: "the race doesn't always go for the swiftest."

Craig Swenson wrote:

> The confirmation bias is the tendency for people to only see what they already believe to be true. When people are ego-invested in a project, the confirmation bias will even be stronger. [110]

Second, intellectual abilities and task relevant ability have both been working to be related to overall group performance. However, the correlation is not particularly high suggesting that other factors, such as the size of the team or group, the type of tasks being performed, the actions of its leaders and level of conflict within the group, also influence performance. As far as student engagement strategies go, acknowledging the effort students have invested in learning looks like an obvious choice. I always start by understanding the things that motivate and inspire my students to keep bettering themselves. Certificates can be the most meaningful of rewards when it comes to motivating adults to learn because they not only want to build their skills, but also to have something to show for it. Consider how completion and achievement can be acknowledged through certificates. It may seem obvious to most of us but I'll say it anyway: creating an effective team, one that gets done what it supposed to get done, doesn't just happen. Yet considering the way many organisations approach teaming, it appears that very often, management just doesn't get it.

Again, Swenson said:

> The team begins its evolution at the point of formation. All team members are together for the first time, and their initial task is to define what they want to accomplish and how they will operate as a team. We have discussed the issue value and method of purposing. We learned that team's members need to validate and clarity the reason why they are coming together and what they hope to accomplish. The team then needs to set goals and establish measures to assure both progress and achievement in the team's work. [111]

For any board to be effective, it is important to have a cohesive group of people who work well together at selection. In purely representational boards, where members elect representatives from their own region or sector, consensus building can be challenging. It is important to seek competent candidates and inform members objectively on the qualifications of candidates and the need to elect qualified board members. It also is in the best interest of the organization to provide orientation and training to all new board members. Board members need to see the association as an entity, not as an agent for their particular constituents.

Adjustments

Both tasks goals and process rules tend to be more made under the team mantle of idealism. As the demand for the task and personalities of team's members unfold, the team needs to clarify and adjust its expectations. Task issues at this point tend to revolving around deadlines and the scope of the work. The needs in my classroom are not always negative. Students, especially young ones, are usually undergoing the process of understanding their skills. However, this is experienced enough to tell that a certain my student has a particular skill or talent. In this case, skills and talents become needs too because they require nurturing to develop. Therefore, once identifies them and provides the essential support to develop them, they help my students to discover and grow them.

Adjustment in ground level rules takes on an internal staff focus. As leadership within the team begins to develop, power and position struggle are not uncommon. Nothing can destroy trust as quickly in a team than to have team discussions shared with those people outside the team. To avoid these areas of problems, team members need to decide how they will represent the organisation to others. Identifying and meeting individual student needs boosts their morale and encourages them. In some cases, my student does not gain much from mass instruction. As such, when provides individually prescribed instruction (IPI) it significantly helps many of my students to understand and grasp educational concepts. This applies more to subjects such as mathematics and art. If student feel supported by their tutor, they develop rather than lose interest in learning. It is very difficult for the team to move forward with focus back to the issue once a personal attribution has been made.

People can differ on issues and still maintain respect and trust. Once the focus is personal, however, both are often lost. In order to realise that value, the team must accept those differing ideas of team members. While the team usually agrees that this is desirable, and even makes ground level rules to reinforce the desire for multiple perspectives, the verbal behaviour of arguing often undoes that intent.

According to Thompson

> Teams whose members are preoccupied with their political image are less effective than are teams whose members do not get caught up in their self-image. This should not be construed to mean that teams should be completely obvious to organisational issues. It is obvious that teams, like individuals, are sensitive to how they are viewed by the organisation and relevant organisational authorities. [112]

The best way for a teacher to organise the classroom is by first identifying the characteristics of each student. My students need more personalised instruction can sit closer to me a teacher. If one of my student's has visual difficulties, I sit him or her closer to the blackboard. They can also sit near a door or window where there is an abundance of light. Evidently, it is paramount that I identify and meet individual student needs when teaching. This is because it allows them to devote their energies beyond regular teaching into effective education that is supportive and considerate for each of my student. In this way, my students are motivated, supported, empowered, and developed because optimum learning conditions are created.

But understanding my own functional skills will help my students improve their personal skills, knowledge and understanding which will hopefully increase their career aspirations and to function effectively and independently from day to day both in life and work. They're also a good learning tool for my students to engage confidently with others, for problem solve in familiar and unfamiliar situations and to help develop personally and professionally as positive citizens who can contribute to (ministerial) society. There student engagement tactics that can make a huge difference to boosting my student's enthusiasm for new knowledge and skills. What's great about these tactics is that they can be applied across different courses. In fact, my student engagement tips can be considered as best practices for motivating every student, no matter the type of training content.

What is the purpose of a team?
The purpose of a team is the reason for the actions they perform in their organization. Well, this depends on the definition you use. It can be a group of people united by a common business goal; a group of people committed to achieving common objectives. Teams can achieve so much and this is the reason so much time and effort is spent on building teams and developing teams. This is what helps keep them aligned and fulfilled toward reaching their company's objectives and goals. The team purpose is why they exist and can motivate employees in their work.

Team building is the process of deliberately creating an effective team by focusing on those factors that support team performance. Common team building activities focus on clarifying roles and goals; building trust, accountability and commitment; improving or designing processes; supporting the use of healthy team norms to encourage effective communication and conflict resolution; and focusing on leadership behaviors. Often, a team-building event will focus on more than one aspect of team-building. At its most comprehensive, team building begins with an assessment process that looks at different areas of team effectiveness and then uses the data to determine the actions. Most commonly, though, team building activities are used as maintenance for an already.

Knowing the purpose of a team is important in giving an organization meaning and direction in their efforts. It is what binds team members together as they work for a common purpose. When individuals know their team's purpose, they can understand how they can make a difference. The purpose of a team is to determine how a unique set of people can use their skills to accomplish a goal at a specific time. A clear team purpose can help motivate individuals into action. However, I am experienced it is important for people to recognise that there is a difference between team building and team development or team working. Team building involves bringing together new teams and giving them a sense of direction, a period of getting to know their colleagues, recognizing skills and abilities. Team development is the next stage, which involves teamworking skills such as sharing ideas, co-operating, being open and supporting one another. A common mistake our students make when they first approach is to confuse the term team building with team working. We believe that if you cannot define the problem, then it is difficult to fix it.

Some benefits of knowing your team include:

1. <u>Discuss your vision regularly:</u> Purposeful teams have regular discussions about their organization's vision. Let your employees know why the company exists and what impact their actions have. For instance, a business may present employees with an annual update that shares their numbers and overall impact for the year.

2. <u>Be open to feedback:</u> To help your team meet its purpose, evaluate behaviors that may be interfering with your performance. Conduct feedback for individuals and the team overall to identify areas of improvement! It can also be helpful for management roles to ask their employees for constructive criticism as well so that they can make adjustments and continue doing what others feel is going well.

3. <u>Participate in team-building activities:</u> In order to understand the effectiveness of your team, consider participating in team-building training activities. Here you can discover how individuals work together and find the strengths and weaknesses of your team. These activities can help foster collaboration in working toward a mutual goal. Setting milestones is a way to work toward accomplishing a team goal. This helps everyone understand what needs to be achieved. Continually keep employees informed about the progress made and what the organization is looking to accomplish next.

4. <u>Consider employee talent:</u> When assembling teams for projects, consider the talent employees exhibit and how they combine with other employees.

This is where a team can be more effective than individual effort since it has resources to multiple skills and levels. During specific projects, select individuals who you feel may work best on it based on their experiences. Seek employees who are purpose-focused when looking to expand your team. To do this, find employees whose values align with your organizations. Those driven by purpose create positive additions to your team when they know what they are working toward. Also look for employees who match the current company culture and would get along with the current employees.

5. Connect the team's purpose with the overall organization: When building your team purpose, connect it with your organization's overall purpose statement. This helps build alignment with the company and helps individuals set their priorities. Consider how your team supports the organization's mission and is part of the bigger team.

Chapter Seven

Types of Communication Theories in the Organizational Setting

Definition of Communication

Communication describes the transmission of ideas between or among persons in a language common to all. Such communication forms a basic ingredient of sound team leadership. In recent years, leaders have become increasingly aware of the significance of solid communication theory in developing satisfactory witnesses for the organisation. This communication is another essential organizational skill to consider. Communication is the key to managing and improving and to appropriate behaviour during organisation sessions of any kinds. To get through a session without any behaviour issues or disruptions would be wonderful, but this very rarely happens. How successfully we share and receive information in the job determines our communication abilities. We'll be able to provide other members of our team with the information they need in an efficient and timely manner if we're an organized leader or communicator.

This chapter deals broadly with the principles and problems of communication as they occur in almost all phases of organisation relationships. The communication process has two main elements, the sender who initiates the message, and the receiver who decodes the message. However, in between this process, the sender encodes the message by choosing a method to compose the message, whether verbal, nonverbal, or written language. The message is then sent through a medium, and as it is received, the receiver then decodes for meaningful information. These elements in the communication process determine the quality of the communication, and as such to ensure effective communication, the dynamics of internal and external communication. Hassall defines communication as:

> Communication is the sharing of information between individuals, which involves identifying, collecting, discussing, interpreting and evaluating the information. This is considered as the central aspect to the success of a team. Lack of communication is therefore a drawback for teams to achieve some if any of their goals. As such there are several ways that can be implemented whether for a short term or long-term period. The strategies used to improve the communication in the team should therefore involve the dynamics relating to both internal and external communication. 113

This general model can help our understanding and perception of almost any aspect of communication. Making improving workplace communication has a big impact on our level of organization. We may communicate more efficiently and reduce the possibilities of miscommunication by scheduling face-to-face meetings, keeping track of key discussions, and drafting efficient emails. Thus, improving work place organized communicators stress efficiency by responding swiftly to inquiries, offering clear directions, and relaying information consistently. We should communicate with our team members on a regular basis my experience over times in studies has helped me identify various aspects and how to deal with them effectively. Providing communication with individual in ways that meet their individual needs sounds easier than it is. Good communication is constructive and specific and does not raise anyone's hackles or result in resistance.

Communication skills refer to your abilities to give and receive information effectively. Being a good communicator involves a number of different skills, but there's a unifying theme between them all: they make working with others much easier and more streamlined. Communication skills have their own section, but being an effective communicator is all about being organized. It's important to keep our team in the loop with our progress on a project, but it's equally important to be a good active listener who understands what's being asked of them and the priorities of various tasks.

According to Moseley:

> Internal communication is communicating within the teams whether formally, informally, vertically or horizontally. This type of communication focuses on promoting effective communication through producing and delivering messages, while creating a channel for feedback, debate or any discussion. [114]

These factors can occur internally or externally and result in poor communication. When team members don't have a mutual understanding, or there is lack of social cohesion, it creates an issue for the team. However, in order to solve a communication issue within the team, the issue has to be analyzed thoroughly. In addition to this there are other risks that are involved in subject specialist area. There is an effective communication within Miller's Bible College and Institution, and also Credited Body and Theological University. These institutions take pains to encode our message clearly at all levels, both vertically and horizontally. They both work with both an Internal Verifier and an External Verifier to confirm that students are academically rigorous while being fair; differentiated, and not putting students under any un-necessary stress (fair deadlines/ preparation/ assessment methods). Some students might not be ready to be observed for a practical skill, or feel so pressured by target dates for a theory test that they resort to colluding or plagiarising work.

No matter where we work or what we do, being able to communicate effectively is a crucial skill. Strong communication skills commonly support highly organized people like what I have seen over the years in different education institutes. Note that communication skills are made up of soft skills. In contrast to hard skills, which must be learned through training, soft skills are acquired throughout our life and relate to our interpersonal abilities and intangible qualities that make working alongside others better.

Kenneth wrote:

> Communication does not take place in a vacuum. We dare not reduce it to a series of words encoded by a source and decoded by a receiver. The total context or environment in

which any message is given and or received
consists of more than words and ideas; it forms
a veritable matrix of human relationships. 115

Constructive communication does not only let our employees
and employers, or teachers and students etc., know what is
right and what is wrong, but provides suggestions on how
individual can approach the various points raised. This is
not the same as telling the individual exactly what he / she
should do; rather it is about sending the individual off in a
certain direction (of thought). This describes the importance
of all staff consistently and fairly applying boundaries and
rules for students and teachers, or employee and employer in
accordance with the policies and procedures of the college
setting. When providing communication there are a number
of things that can help made my feedback a constructive
communication for an individual. These are:

Being specific: For example, if my communication
information is missing, then it helps to state what is missing
and where exactly. It also helps to give examples in the
individual's work.

Constructive communication: this refers to building up
provides refers to building up matter rather than breaking
it down. This type of criticism makes the other person feel
that you really want them to improve. For instance, being a
teacher mostly gives feedback to my students so that they
put in extra effort in order to improve their presentations
potential skills or assignments. Also, constructive feedback
is not always positive rather it can be focused on the areas
where improvement is required.

Relevant: Communication in general always be relevant to the lesson. It is ideally customised for each single student who is completing an activity even if it is in a group. When individuals are presenting in a group, first the group should be judged over the areas for general improvement, then individually each member should be given feedback on their own performance.

Immediate: Moreover, constructive communication can be immediate and spontaneous. An immediate response is much more effective than one given later. This may be because many individuals will remember the reaction of their organisation teacher where they positively or negatively comment over their work. If the communication is late, our individuals might not be able to relate it directly with the action.

Factual: Communication under any circumstances should not be biased. Negativity, anger or disappointment can be portrayed by tone of voice, body language and facial expressions. This can be very demotivating for any individual students of any subject, age or ethnic background. The comments made by employers should never personally attack our employees, especially in a public setting. It should rather be related to the learning outcomes and assessment criteria directly. All aspects of giving communication should be professional and within legal guidelines. If two different organisations management are assessing or teaching the same group of individuals, they will have to follow the same curriculum for marking them. This is also known as standardisation.

<u>Helpful:</u> Constructive communication can help individuals in improving their quality of work, rather than being belittling them. For instance, communication regarding a presentation which was presented in class can make an individual feel disrespected or ashamed. Thus, to avoid this, we should make sure that we call that particular individual separately and talk to him or her about the problem observed during the assessment or activity. Moreover, we should remember that whatever words we use during our communication, everyone has the right to be respected. This is where we have patience in letting the individual know about their mistake and the way it should be.

It might be worth considering a different technique or activity or rephrasing the communication if the error is being repeated. This would be a sign that the communication is being received or understood. While for Tankosic, Ivetic and Mikelic have given this useful explanation on external communication:

> External communication on the other hand is any information learnt and brought from outside of the team. Both types of communication involve activities to manage communication internally or externally with the aim of creating and improving communication within the team. 116

This will allow the issues being faced to be highlighted and as such recognize team efforts in reaching objectives. In applying this model team members will therefore be grouped with tasks in regards to who knows how to do what. The Ministry of Education would have displayed a more mechanistic structure before the Corona Virus pandemic, having a strict hierarchy of authority, with a simple but formalized way of vertical communication. However, the technological changes during the pandemic lockdown have impacted this structure making it more organic. This can be seen through the way in which communication now takes place, not just between the people, but between the ministries. The ministries now tend to work together more closely due to this change to be able to fit the technological wants and needs being demanded by the people. This has created a decentralized structure to ensure that these demands of the people and the economy are being met.

Due to the current pandemic, Covid-19, there has been several technological transformations in the economy, which involve the increase in technological use as well as the demand for more technology to facilitate workers and students during the pandemic lockdown. The Ministry of Education is the Government's advisory system for change, growth, and development in education. This system provides the legislative framework, policies, strategies, plans, and resources required for educational purposes. The Ministry of Education is one of the main ministries affected by the pandemic, which have resulted in the closing of schools, and an increase in demand for technology usage. There will therefore be a technological change, which will require a change in the organizational structure to facilitate the people's wants and needs, as well as the Ministry itself.

These made all our individual organisation members to ensure are included and can participate, and will enable them to assess that learning is taking place by the rightful communication. Ideally, a good communication should have a beginning, middle and ending. We think of this as the introduction, development and conclusion of communication with our members. We have also created and / or use relevant resources to bring our subject to life. Many of our organisational members, like college with learning disabilities (LD) often have difficulty with language. This difficulty takes many forms. They might have trouble understanding what we say. This study will make the result of auditory problems (difficulty processing sounds) or receptive language difficulties (trouble understanding the words and turning them into action or pictures). Our organisations members with LD may also have difficulty speaking due to trouble forming their thoughts, attaching words to concepts, putting words in the right order, and many other reasons.

These language–based difficulties are compounded when college staffs and members with learning disabilities those who are not English language learners. This article will make some suggestions for making our college organisation more inviting for all staffs and members who have difficulties with language. Here are some of my suggestions:

a. While it is important for you to speak naturally, you should recognize that if you are sarcastic, some of your staff and members in your organisation may not understand your intended meaning. Therefore, we use words slowly, clearly, and naturally. If our pace tends to be fast, focus on ensuring that each syllable is clear, rather than trying to speak slowly.

Try using shorter sentences. Ask our staffs and members to signal us if we are speaking too quickly.

b. Face our staffs and members and avoid putting our hand in front of our face. People sometimes want to see the face and lips of person they are struggling to understand.

c. Where practical, turn off machines that create background noise. For example, if one of my neon lights is making a loud buzz, ask maintenance to fix it. Ask administrators to avoid placing organisations with our staffs and members with learning disabilities next to noisy organisations such as the gym.

d. Be careful when we use idioms such as "caught with our pants down" or "back seat driver." Our staffs and members with LD, especially those who are English language staffs and members, may not understand these expressions or may take them literally. Our ELL staffs and members may also have reactions to these phrases that are specific to their culture.

e. Tone of voice, facial expression and gestures may be misunderstood by our staffs and members with learning disabilities (LD). Staffs and members with LD often have difficulty processing these signals. Those who are English language individuals also come from different cultures, so a gesture might have a different meaning for them. While it is important for me to speak naturally, recognize that if you are sarcastic, some of our staffs and members in our organisation may not understand my intended meaning. Use words to reinforce our body language when we need help the class to know how we feel.

f. When we ask a person with a learning disability a question, they will often hesitate before they answer the question because they need to make sure they have heard the words in order, and they need to translate the words into concepts. In addition, they may need time to form their thoughts and turn them into words. We allow a silent period between my question and their answer. We do not give hints or answer the question for them until they show or say that they need help, etc.

Verbal communication Discriminative listening

Verbal communication involves the spoken word, if you or partner's end of the conversation, you have to make an impact. Discriminative listening is first developed at a very early age – perhaps even before birth, in the womb. This is the most basic form of listening and does not involve the understanding of the meaning of words or phrases but merely the different sounds that are produced. In early childhood, for example, a distinction is made between the sounds of the voices of the parents – the voice of the father sounds different to that of the mother. Things like tone, diction, and pacing are all important when you're a speaker. It's also about reading your audience and adjusting these things in real-time to make yourself better understood.

Being an effective verbal communicator is also about being a good listener. It doesn't matter if you give the most eloquent speech in the world if you haven't responded to the right elements of your partner's end of the conversation. Discriminative listening develops through childhood and into adulthood. As we grow older and develop and gain more life experience, our ability to distinguish between different sounds is improved. Not only can we recognise different voices, but we also develop the ability to recognise subtle differences in the way that sounds are made – this is fundamental to ultimately understanding what these sounds mean. Differences include many subtleties, recognising foreign languages, distinguishing between regional accents and clues to the emotions and feelings of the speaker.

Being able to distinguish the subtleties of sound made by somebody who is happy or sad, angry or stressed, for example, ultimately adds value to what is actually being said and, of course, does aid comprehension members to learn from each other once we are not able to understand you. Some of our staff and members when discriminative listening skills are combined with visual stimuli, the resulting ability to 'listen' to body-language enables us to begin to understand the speaker more fully – for example recognising somebody is sad despite what they are saying or how they are saying it.

Skills in verbal communication are special vital for anyone who regularly performs tasks over the phone because you don't get the same nonverbal cues that folks who meet face-to-face have. Still, almost every job involves talking to people at some point, whether it's supervisors, employees, colleagues, distributors, or clients. This relates to the things we say, and while it only comprises 7% of communication, it is still important. We need to assess the conversation to decide how to proceed. For example, we would use short sentences and speak slowly to a child, and do the same to colleagues when trying to explain a complicated work process!

Nothing could be further from the truth. In fact, by taking the time to incorporate these strategies into our working, it will help many more staffs and members become engaged, active participants. This includes not only this college staffs and members with LD, but other staffs and members as well. For example, all English language learners, even those without learning disabilities, will benefit from strategies that focus on making language clearer and more comprehensible. Although incorporating these suggestions may take some extra effort, we will find that practice will make it easier. We may have to plan ahead more, but using these strategies will enable all our staffs and member to learn from each other once were not able to understand you. Some of our staffs and member who were excluded from our management will be included. And that is what good teaching is all about.

Nonverbal communication Comprehensive listening
Things like posture, eye contact, gestures, handshakes, and facial expressions are all part of nonverbal communication. In order to be able use comprehensive listening and therefore gain understanding the listener first needs appropriate vocabulary and language skills. Using overly complicated language or technical jargon, therefore, can be a barrier to comprehensive listening. Comprehensive listening is further complicated by the fact that two different people listening to the same thing may understand the message in two different ways. This problem can be multiplied in a group setting, like a classroom or business meeting where numerous different meanings can be derived from what has been said.

Comprehensive listening is complimented by sub-messages from non-verbal communication, such as the tone of voice, gestures and other body language. These non-verbal signals can greatly aid communication and comprehension but can also confuse and potentially lead to misunderstanding. In many listening situations it is vital to seek clarification and use skills such as reflection aid comprehension. Listeners take all this into account when they're in the process of parsing out the information we're delivering. A confident stance, direct eye contact, and a relaxed face will exhibit confidence and make listeners more prone to accept the spoken information.

Nonverbal communication skills are difficult to show off on a resume or cover letter, so we'll have to wait for the interview stage to show off our acuity. Although all types of listening are 'active' – they require concentration and a conscious effort to understand. Informational listening is less active than many of the other types of listening. When we're listening to learn or be instructed, we are taking in new information and facts, we are not criticising or analysing. Informational listening, especially in formal settings like in work meetings or while in education, is often accompanied by note taking – a way of recording key information so that it can be reviewed later.

In terms of planning, we feel we are fairly strong with creating an effective scheme of work to account for all our student's needs. One area that we certainly need to build up is the extension tasks we can implement to stretch our higher achieving students. Although we plan for a task like this, we rarely plan for what if that task is achieved? It is a question we have since started to ask myself 'what next?' This will ensure that our student progression is maximised during the lesson rather than we have completed that and consolidate. Mohammed and Dumville claimed that:

> With the use of this model, team effectiveness which is surrounded by the basis of communication, will improve if team members have a shared understanding of the task, team and issues. After implementing this model, a transitive memory system will then be developed in the team. [117]

They will continue to reflect on this process and ensure that they remain adaptable as each year and will gain new students with new challenges and we must ensure we can adapt to those to create the best learning environment for them to thrive in. All the Teachers at Miller's Bible College and Institution believe and understand that all their students ought to acquire equal hopes, education and future aspirations from their learning. On the other hand, being a student, I have met many students with different dynamics during their studies career. The main difference is that some students will learn fast, and others will be slower; that are challenged or disabled in some way. In the light of this, it was crucial that all the teachers identify and meet the needs of every student without discrimination.

Written Communication Critical Listening
Being able to write clearly and concisely is valuable in just about every position. We can be said to be engaged in critical listening when the goal is to evaluate or scrutinise what is being said. Critical listening is a much more active behaviour than informational listening and usually involves some sort of problem solving or decision making. Critical

listening is akin to critical reading; both involve analysis of the information being received and alignment with what we already know or believe. Whereas informational listening may be mostly concerned with receiving facts and / or new information - critical listening is about analysing opinion and making a judgement.

When the word 'critical' is used to describe listening, reading or thinking it does not necessarily mean that we are claiming that the information we are listening to is somehow faulty or flawed. Rather, critical listening means engaging in what we are listening to by asking ourselves questions such as, 'what is the speaker trying to say?' or 'what is the main argument being presented?', 'how does what we have hearing differ from my beliefs, knowledge or opinion?'. Critical listening is, therefore, fundamental to true learning.

Much of the communication within and between businesses is done through email, so knowing how to write in a way that strikes a good tone while being professional and delivering information in an easy-to-understand way is a true skill. Written communication skills are the skills we use to convey messages in writing. Writing is one of the primary modes of business communication as it's used to offer detailed instructions, provide information and relay suggestions or ideas. These skills allow us to write lengthy or complex messages that all recipients can read and understand.

Don't fall into the trap of thinking technology is damaging our communication skills! Use it to improve them. Communicating through text, email, and social media is a good way to get things moving or to keep a conversation going; although nothing beats face-to-face meetings for getting to the heart of a matter. In a way, this could relate to gesticulating wildly with our arms while pulling funny faces! However, it is normally used to describe making presentations at work. Good visual communication skills allow us to get our point across in a handful of PowerPoint slides.

We'll need written communication skills for both internal and external communications. When addressing internal business employees, we might use notice boards, emails, reports, instant messages, bulletins, employee manuals and memos. We might use telegrams, contracts, brochures, advertisements, postcards, emails, faxes, proposals, letters, websites and news releases when addressing external parties. Being a good leader means communicating in a way that projects confidence and motivates others. Good leaders take into account the skill sets, needs, and work styles of their team members.

While we may think written communication falls under the nonverbal category, most HR managers differentiate between the two, seeing as written communication plays such a large role in day-to-day operations at most companies. Many day-to-day decisions that we make are based on some form of 'critical' analysis, whether it be critical listening, reading or thought. Our opinions, values and beliefs are based on our ability to process information and formulate our own feelings about the world around us as well as weigh up the pros and cons to make an informed decision.

Excellent talent in written communication is easy to show off on a resume and cover letter. If we can persuade hiring managers that we're a top candidate based on nothing but these documents, we've proved we have a knack for written communication. It is often important, when listening critically, to have an open-mind and not be biased by stereotypes or preconceived ideas. By doing this we will become a better listener and broaden our knowledge and perception of other people and our relationships. Start by taking stock of what we're naturally good at. Ask friends, family, or colleagues – we might be surprised to hear where they believe our strengths lie. Then consider some difficult moments at work and think of how poor communication (ours or our colleagues) led to disastrous results. Contemplate which communicative skills could have resolved that situation in a better way.

Improving Our Staffs and Member Communication Skills

These 7 tips have helped me over the years in studies and improving my communication skills. Build better speakers and writers of tomorrow by challenging ourselves to think critically, listen actively, and work together special at Miller's Bible College and Institution.

1. Watch the Power Point - Model Conversation Skills.
Conversation is one of the most basic and essential communication skills. It enables people to share thoughts, opinions, and ideas, and receive them in turn. Although it may appear simple on the surface, effective conversations include a give-and-take exchange that consists of elements such as:

    a. body language
    b. eye contact
    c. summarizing
    d. paraphrasing
    e. responding

Students can learn the foundational elements of conversation by watching PowerPoint or videos of these interactions taking place. Pause the video and ask questions such as, "What message is the listener sending by crossing his arms? What else can we tell by observing the expressions and body language of both people in the conversation?"

2. Use Technology.
From audio books to apps, there is a multitude of technological resources we can use for improving student communication skills. Students can listen to or read along with audio books to hear how the speaker pronounces and enunciates different words or phrases. Some great free apps that improve student communication skills are voice thread.

3. Reinforce Active Listening.
Communication isn't just about speaking; it's also about listening. As a student at Miller's Bible College and Institution, we can help students develop listening skills by reading a selection of text aloud, and then having the class discusses and reflects on the content. This makes the active listening skills also means listening to understand rather than reply. By me reinforce building good listening skills by encouraging students to practice asking clarifying questions to fully understand the speaker's intended message.

4. Group Presentations and Assignments.
Our team building exercises can also help students sharpen both oral and written communication skills. Not only does it offer students the chance to work in small groups, thereby reducing some of the pressure, but it also gives them the opportunity to debate their opinions, take turns, and work together towards a common goal.

5. Use Tasks and Activities That Foster Critical Thinking.
Another task-based method that I can use for improving student communication skills is through critical thinking exercises. These can be done verbally or through written assignments that give students the chance to answer questions creatively using their own words and expressions. Get a head start with the communication-based critical thinking activities and games in our most popular resource, the critical thinking companion.

6. Reflective Learning Opportunities.
Recording students reading selected text or videotaping group presentations is an excellent method for assessing their communication strengths and weaknesses. This made students can reflect on their oral performance in small groups. Then, ask each student to critique the others so that they can get used to receiving constructive criticism.

7. Find Teachable Moments.
Whatever the age group we are working with, maximize on the everyday happenings in the classroom environment. For example, if a student answers a question in a complicated way, we might ask that they rephrase what they said, or challenge the class to ask clarifying questions. If an unfamiliar word pops up in a text or on a film, pause in order for the class to search for the word in the dictionary.

Conclusion

In this study I have portrayed the formulation of management strategy as a complex process involving the consideration of environmental and organisational factors as well as management values and organisation politics. The major theme of this book and of the series, of which it forms a part, is that businesses are complex. They cannot be understood by reference to their activities alone. These activities, which include innovation, finance and accounting and so on, take place in a series of contexts. It is my intention that they can only be understood fully when those contexts within which they operate are also understood. It is also my intention to show that the relationships between business activities in these contexts are dynamic.

As a result the processes, including a consideration of management values and negotiations between interested parties. Today's organisations are reeling from the human impacts of the changes that have been forced on them by technology, international competition, and demographics. The effective management of people takes place in the context of the wider environmental setting, including the changing patterns of organisations and attitudes to work. It is frequently documented that a global economy, increased business competitiveness, the move towards more customer-driven markets, advances in scientific knowledge, especially telecommunications, office automation and the downsizing of organisations have led to a period of constant change and the need for greater organisational flexibility.

Jobs are becoming a series of short-term contracts and a large majority of workers believe a job for life no longer exists and are concerned about job security. Organisations even the Churches are making increasing use of group or team approaches to work with an emphasis on cooperation, participation and empowerment. The power and influence of private and public organisations, the rapid spread of new technology, and the impact of various socio- economic and political factors have given rise to the concept of corporate social responsibilities and business ethics. This is why transition management is such a critical skill for you to develop. You are going to find yourself dealing with the aftermath of mismanaged or unmanaged transition every time you turn around. That aftermath is a manager's nightmare.

Competence is a critical variable for the achievement of both individual and organisational success. It implies either an immediate or potential capability to reach a high standard of performance. As human resource strategy becomes more influential, performance management is more closely integrated with overall business performance. Strategists emphasise the core competences of organisations which are made up of the individual competences of its staff. As with management by objectives, competence requirements and goals can be cascaded from the top so that all employees are performing in an integrated fashion.

I have identified a range of approaches and styles, which may operate at the same time, although at different stages of the firm's development one type of strategy may be more appropriate than another. Every person is capable of making mistake in his or her perception or judgement of events or people. It is possible to identify the more important perceptual errors which can be made. Throughout the book examples to illustrate points made will be given from both the private sector and where appropriate from the public service. This project has been developed to encourage management to formulate new attitudes towards understanding the significance of "How to Manage Human Resource".

Affording the right skills is an extremely important duty of management. The providing an environment whereby the right skills can be either taught or developed is quite a wide ranging management responsibility. Everyone in the organisation should feel a sense of 'ownership' of and participation in the acquisition of these skills. It is the job of vigilant management to ensure that these mistakes are avoided. This could be potentially difficult for any new manager that has not previously managed a team and this was not an ethos of local management control. This provides the flexibility to focus on individual professional development and ensure the team works as an efficient, dynamic, complementary workforce.

It might be concluded that unsuccessful organisations are those which do not react to the needs and demands of their customers, who do not anticipate the skills and abilities of their competitors and who do not adapt to changes in technology. Finally it is possible to introduce programmes which both emphasise the quality dimension and also introduce best practice in management generally.

As many academic and professional courses move towards examining through 'real life situations', it is essential that the application of management theory to real life situations receive some attention. Sceptical that so much could have come from a series of information conversations I visited the company of all them and met a cross- section of those who worked there. What I have done here is to write in a slightly paraphrased form the substance of our conversations. I hope that you will find this book equally useful. Its message is both simple and important.

References

1. Ann Gravells, The Award in Education and Training Revised Edition, SAGE, London: SAGE Publication Ltd, 2014

2. A. Hudson, D. Hayes and T. Andrew, Working Lives in 1990s, London: Global Futures, 1996

3. Dick Benjamin, Jim Durkin, Dick Iverson and Terry Edwards, The Master Builder, Christian Equippers International, South Lake Tahoe: California, 1985

4. Laurie J. Mullins, Management and Organisational Behaviour Sixth Edition, London: Prentice Hall, Financial Times, 2002

5. Dick Benjamin, Jim Durkin, Dick Iverson and Terry Edwards, The Master Builder, Christian Equippers International, South Lake Tahoe: California, 1985

6. Ann Gravells, The Award in Education and Training Revised Edition, SAGE, London: SAGE Publication Ltd, 2014

7. Laurie J. Mullins, Management and Organisational Behaviour Sixth Edition, London: Prentice Hall, Financial Times, 2002

8. Ibid.

9. D. Smith, Crossing the Private – Public Divide, Management Today, August 1998

10. Kenneth O. Gangel, Team Leadership in Christian Ministry, Chicago: Moody Press, 1997

11. Ibid.

12. Laurie J. Mullins, Management and Organisational Behaviour Sixth Edition, London: Prentice Hall, Financial Times, 2002

13. Robert H. Welch, Job Descriptions that Work, May/June, Unknown Publisher, 1995

14. Dick Benjamin, Jim Durkin, Dick Iverson and Terry Edwards, The Master Builder, Christian Equippers International, South Lake Tahoe: California, 1985

15. Hrand Faxenian, Effective Communication in Small Plants: Management Aids, Unknown Publisher, 2006

16. Kenneth O. Gangel, Team Leadership in Christian Ministry, Chicago: Moody Press, 1997

17. Kenneth O. Gangel, Team Leadership in Christian Ministry, Chicago: Moody Press, 1997

18. Dick Benjamin, Jim Durkin, Dick Iverson and Terry Edwards, The Master Builder, Christian Equippers International, South Lake Tahoe: California, 1985

19. Mike Haralambos, Martin Holborn, The Fourth Edition of Sociology: Themes and Perspective, London: Harper Collins Educational Publishers, 1995

20. J. R. Lewicki, B. Barry, M.D. Saunders, Essentials of negotiation, Boston, Mass: McGraw-Hill, 2007

21. F. Lunenburg, (2012). Mechanistic-Organic Organization-An Axiomatic Theory: Authority Based on Bureaucracy or Professional Norms. http://pdfs.semanticscholar.org/b657/87be6d50ce5d5133de399268b075f7b03604.pdf

22. Peter Blau, The Dynamics of Bureaucracy Second Edition, Chicago: University of Chicago Press, 1974

23. Laurie J. Mullins, Management and Organisational Behaviour Sixth Edition, London: Prentice Hall, Financial Times, 2002

24. P. F. Drucker, The Practice of Management, (unknown city), Heinemann Professional, 1989

25. David Needle, Business in Context: An Introduction to Business and its Environment, London: Chapman and Hall Published, 1995

26. R. Stewart, The Reality of Management, (unknown city), Butterworth- Heinemann, 1999

27. L. J. Mullins, Management and Organisational Behaviour, London: Prentice Hall, 2002

28. John Adair, Not Bosses but Leaders, London: Kogan Page, 2006

29. Tony Dawson, Principles and Practice: Modern Management, Kent, Tudor Business Publishing Limited, 1993

30. Editors Chris Clegg, Karen Legge and Susan Walsh, The Experience of Managing: A Skills Guide, London: Macmillan Business Press Ltd, 1999

31. O. Lundy and A. Cowling, Strategic Human Resource Management, (unknown city and Publishers), 1996

32. R. Stewart, The Reality of Management, Third Edition, London: Butterworth Heinemann, 1999

33. Tony Dawson, Principles and Practice: Modern Management, Kent, Tudor Business Publishing Limited, 1993

34. Editors Chris Clegg, Karen Legge and Susan Walsh, The Experience of Managing: A Skills Guide, London: Macmillan Business Press Ltd, 1999

35. L. Urwick, The Elements of Administration, London: Pitman, 1947

36. J. Child, Organisation: A Guide to Problems and Practice, (unknown city), Paul Chapman, 1988

37. L. Urwick, The Elements of Administration, London: Pitman, 1947

38. R. Townsend, Further up the Organisation, London: Coronet Books, 1985
39. I. Worthington and C Britton, The Business Environment, third edition, London: Financial Times, Prentice Hall, 2000
40. Laurie J. Mullins, Management and Organisational Behaviour Sixth Edition, London: Prentice Hall, Financial Times, 2002
41. David Needle, Business in Context: An Introduction to Business and its Environment, London: Chapman and Hall Published, 1995
42. W. French and C. Bell, Organisation Development: Behavioural Science Interventions for Organisation Improvement, London: Prentice Hall, 1999
43. L. Mullins, Management and Organisational Behaviour, London: Prentice Hall, 2002
44. Ibid.
45. Tony Dawson, Principles and Practice: Modern Management, Kent, Tudor Business Publishing Limited, 1993
46. Ibid.
47. Collins Concise Dictionary 21st Century Edition (Ed) J. M. Sinclair, Glasgow: Harper Collins Publishers, 2001
48. W. L. French and C. H. Bell, Organisation Development: Behaviour Science Interventions for Organisation Improvement, sixth edition, London: Prentice Hall, 1999
49. Cameron, K & Quinn, R. (1989). Diagnosing and Changing Organizational Culture: Based on the Competing Values Framework
50. M. Alam (2019), Bureaucratic Culture, Empowering Leadership, Affective Commitment, and Knowledge

Sharing Behaviour in Indonesian Government Public Services... http://tandfonline.com/doi/full/10.1080/23311975.2019.1680099

51. A. Moorhouse, (2020), The Importance of Adaptability Skills in the Workplace. Retrieved from http://trainingjournal.com/articles/features/importance-adaptability-skills-workplace

52. Craig Swenson, Tools for Teams: Building Effective Teams in the Workplace, Boston: MA., Pearson Custom Publishing Lit., 2001

53. A. Kransdorff, 'History – A Powerful Management Tool': Administrator, London, (unknown Publisher), 1991

54. David Needle, Business in Context: An Introduction to Business and its Environment, London: Chapman and Hall Published, 1995

55. Peter Leyland and Terry Woods, Textbook on Administrative Law, London: Blackstone Press Limited, 1997

56. Tony Dawson, Principles and Practice: Modern Management, Kent, Tudor Business Publishing Limited, 1993

57. Peter Leyland and Terry Woods, Textbook on Administrative Law, London: Blackstone Press Limited, 1997

58. George B. Weber, "Growing Tomorrow's Leaders": The Leader of the Future, San Francisco: Jossey Bass, 1996

59. Lawrence O. Richards, "Theology of Servant Leadership: A Response", Christian Education Journal 9, Unknown city: Winter 1989

60. Laurie J. Mullins, Management and Organisational Behaviour Sixth Edition, London: Prentice Hall, Financial Times, 2002

61. G. White, Employee Commitment, ACAS Work Research Unit, October 1987

62. W. Altman, C. Cooper, and A. Garner, New Deal Need to Secure Commitment: London: Professional Manager, September 1999

63. P. F. Drucker, The Practice of Management, London: Butterworth Heinemann, 1989

64. George Strauss and Leonard Sayles, Personnel: The Human Problems of Management, Englewood Cliffs: New York, 1960

65. Abraham Zaleznik, Human Dilemmas of Leadership, New York: Harper and Row, 1966

66. F. Wilson, Organisational Behaviour: A Critical Introduction, Oxford University Press, 1999

67. R. Stewart, The Reality of Management, Third Edition, London: Butterworth Heinemann, 1999

68. R. Heller, In Search of European Excellence, Harper Collins Business, 1997

69. Laurie J. Mullins, Management and Organisational Behaviour Sixth Edition, London: Prentice Hall, Financial Times, 2002

70. Ronald R. Sims. 2002. Managing Organizational Behaviour. London. – Textbook/organizational-theory-3/behavioral-perspectives-30/the-behavioral-science- approach-174-8382/ 10

71. Ibid.

72. P. T. Costa, & R. R. McCrae, Five Factors are Basic: Personality and Individual Differences, Unknown Publishers and city, 1992

73. Ibid.

74. Laurie J. Mullins, Management and Organisational Behaviour Sixth Edition, London: Prentice Hall, Financial Times, 2002

75. Peter Senge, The Fifth Discipline, New York: Doubleday, 1990

76. Michael Armstrong, How to be an Even Better Manager, tenth edition, London: Kogan Page Publishers, 2017

77. A. Mumford, Individual and Organisational Learning: The Pursuit of Change, Routledge: The Open University, 1994

78. Holly McGurgan, Career Trend, October 09, 2019 – advertise@careertrend.com

79. B. Garratt, Learning to Lead, Unknown city, Fontana, 1991

80. Michael Armstrong, How to be an Even Better Manager, tenth edition, London: Kogan Page Publishers, 2017

81. D. Kola, Organisation Psychology: An Experiential Approach to Organisational Behaviour, London: Prentice Hall, 1984

82. Laurie Mullins, management and Organisational Behaviour, London: Prentice Hall, 2002

83. Michael Armstrong, How to be an Even Better Manager, tenth edition, London: Kogan Page Publishers, 2017

84. Allan P. Miller, Explaining Time Management, London, All Nations Bible College and School of Theological Studies, October, 2021

85. S. Crainer, Key Management Ideas: Thinkers that Changed the Management World, London: Financial Times Prentice Hall, 1998

86. Della Thompson (ed), The Concise Oxford Dictionary of Current English, London: BCA, 1996

87. David Needle, Business in Context: An Introduction to Business and its Environment, London: Chapman and Hall Published, 1995

88. L. J. Mullins, Management and Organisational Behaviour, London: Prentice Hall, 2002

89. David Needle, Business in Context: An Introduction to Business and its Environment, London: Chapman and Hall Published, 1995

90. Christian Fisher, Career Trend, July 05, 2017 – advertise@careertrend.com

91. Holly McGurgan, Career Trend, October 09, 2019 – advertise@careertrend.com

92. Scott Morgan, Career Trend, July 05, 2017 – advertise@careertrend.com

93. Rob Yeung, Confidence, Harlow: Prentice Hall Life, 2011

94. D. Goleman, Leadership That Gets Results, New York: Harvard Business Reviews, April, 2000

95. Michael Armstrong, How to be an Even Better Manager, tenth edition, London: Kogan Page Publishers, 2017

96. Ibid.

97. Rosabeth Moss Kanter, The Change Master's, London. Allen and Unwin, 1984

98. Michael Armstrong, How to be an Even Better Manager, tenth edition, London: Kogan Page Publishers, 2017

99. M. A. West, Developing Creativity in Organisation, unknown city: BPS, 1997

100. J. Wilson, Buildings Teams with Attitudes: Professional Manager, unknown city and unknown Publishers, 1998
101. R. P. Vecchio, Organisational Behaviour: Core Concepts, unknown city, Dryden Press, 2000
102. Michael Armstrong, How to be an Even Better Manager, tenth edition, London: Kogan Page Publishers, 2017
103. Kenneth O. Gangel, Team Leadership in Christian Ministry, Chicago: The Moody Bible Institute of Chicago, 1997
104. George B. Weber, "Growing Tomorrow's Leaders": The Leader of the Future, San Francisco: Jossey-Bass, 1996
105. Larry Crabb, Connecting: Healing for Ourselves and Our Relationships, London: Word Publishing, 1997
106. Larry Osborne, The Unity Factor, Waco: Tex, Word Publisher, 1989
107. Harold Longenecker, Growing Leaders by Design, Grand Rapids: Kregel Resources, 1995
108. R. M. Belbin, Team Roles at Work, London: Butterworth Heinemann, 1993
109. Craig Swenson, Tools for Teams: Buildings Effective Teams in the Workplace, Boston: Ma., Pearson Custom Publishing 2001
110. Ibid.
111. Ibid.
112. Ibid.
113. S. Hassall, (2009), The Relationship Between Communication and Team Performance: Testing Moderators and Identifying Communication Profiles in Established Work Teams. https://eprints.qut.edu.au/30311/1/Stacey_Hassall_Thesis.pdf

114. C. Moseley, (2019), 7 Reasons Why Internal Communication is Important, Retrieved from https://blog.jostle.me/blog/why-is-internal-communications-important

115. Kenneth O. Gangel, Team Leadership in Christian Ministry, Chicago: The Moody Bible Institute of Chicago, 1997

116. M. Tankosic, P. Ivetic, and K. Mikelic, (2017), Managing Internal and External Communication in a Competitive Climate via EDI Concept, https://pdfs.semanticscholar.org/e4e6/3cca6b3411f97dc312119cbbc155f6461704.pdf

117. S. Mohammed, and B. Dumville, (2001), Team Mental Models in a Team Knowledge Framework: Expanding Theory and Measurement across Disciplinary Boundaries, Retrieved from https://www.jstor.org/stable/3649584?seq=1

Lightning Source UK Ltd.
Milton Keynes UK
UKHW010122240223
417570UK00001B/14